◐ Shortcut

MILAN & THE LAKES

By Michelle Schoenung
and Donald Strachan

Published by
Frommer Media LLC

Copyright © 2016 by Frommer Media LLC. All rights reserved. No part of this publication may be reproduced, stored in a retrieval system, or transmitted in any form or by any means, electronic, mechanical, photocopying, recording, scanning or otherwise, except as permitted under Sections 107 or 108 of the 1976 United States Copyright Act, without the prior written permission of the Publisher. Requests to the Publisher for permission should be addressed to Support@FrommerMedia.com.

Frommer's is a registered trademark of Arthur Frommer. Frommer Media LLC is not associated with any product or vendor mentioned in this book.

ISBN 978-1-62887-258-3 (paper), 978-1-62887-259-0 (e-book)
Editorial Director: Pauline Frommer
Editor: Holly Hughes
Production Editor: Kevin Cristaldi
Cartographer: Liz Puhl
Photo Editor: Dana Davis and Meghan Lamb

For information on our other products or services, see www.frommers.com. Frommer Media LLC also publishes its books in a variety of electronic formats. Some content that appears in print may not be available in electronic formats.

Manufactured in China

5 4 3 2 1

HOW TO CONTACT US

In researching this book, we discovered many wonderful places—hotels, restaurants, shops, and more. We're sure you'll find others. Please tell us about them, so we can share the information with your fellow travelers in upcoming editions. If you were disappointed with a recommendation, we'd love to know that, too. Please write to: Support@FrommerMedia.com

FROMMER'S STAR RATINGS SYSTEM

Every hotel, restaurant and attraction listed in this guide has been ranked for quality and value. Here's what the stars mean:

★ Recommended
★★ Highly Recommended
★★★ A must! Don't miss!

CONTENTS

AN IMPORTANT NOTE

The world is a dynamic place. Hotels change ownership, restaurants hike their prices, museums alter their opening hours, and busses and trains change their routings. And all of this can occur in the several months after our authors have visited, inspected, and written about, these hotels, restaurants, museums and transportation services. Though we have made valiant efforts to keep all our information fresh and up-to-date, some few changes can inevitably occur in the periods before a revised edition of this guidebook is published. So please bear with us if a tiny number of the details in this book have changed. Please also note that we have no responsibility or liability for any inaccuracy or errors or omissions, or for inconvenience, loss, damage, or expenses suffered by anyone as a result of assertions in this guide.

ABOUT THE AUTHORS

Michelle Schoenung is an American journalist and translator in Milan who relocated to Belpaese in 2000 for what was to be a yearlong adventure. Sixteen years on, she is pleased that Milan has evolved into a much more international and cosmopolitan city and has shed its image of merely being a foggy northern Italian business hub. Her writings and translations have appeared in magazines and books in the United States and Italy. In her free time she likes to read, run, travel, cook, and explore the city with her two rambunctious Italian-American sons.

Donald Strachan is a travel journalist who has written about Italy for publications worldwide, including "National Geographic Traveler," "The Guardian," "Sunday Telegraph," CNN.com, and many others. He has also written several Italy guidebooks for Frommer's, including "Frommer's EasyGuide to Rome, Florence, and Venice." For more, see www.donaldstrachan.com.

1

INTRODUCTION

Milan

Milan is the glitzy capital of Lombardy (Lombardia), Italy's most prosperous region. Its factories largely fuel the Italian economy, and its attractions—high fashion, fine dining, hopping dance clubs, and da Vinci's *Last Supper*—have much to offer the visitor. But there's much more than a sophisticated city to Lombardy. To the north, the region bumps up against craggy mountains in a romantic lake district, and to the south it spreads out in fertile farmlands fed by the mighty Po and other rivers.

Lombardy has a different feel from the rest of Italy. The *Lombardi*, who descended from one of the Germanic tribes that overran the Roman empire, and who have over the centuries been ruled by feudal dynasties from Spain, Austria, and France, are a little more Continental than their neighbors to the south; indeed, the *Lombardi* are faster talking, faster paced, and more business-oriented. They even dine differently, tending to eschew olive oil for butter and often forgoing pasta for polenta and risotto.

The Italian lakes have entranced writers from Catullus to Ernest Hemingway. Backed by the Alps and ringed by lush gardens and verdant forests, each has its own charms and, accordingly, its own enthusiasts. Not least among these charms is their easy

PREVIOUS PAGE: **Sforza Castle in Milan.**

accessibility from many Italian cities, making them ideal for short retreats: Lake Maggiore and Lake Como are both less than an hour from Milan, and Lake Garda is tantalizingly close to Venice and Verona. Each of these world-renowned resorts—Como (the choicest), Maggiore (speckled with elegant islands), and Garda (a windsurfing hot spot, and microcosm of Italy, with the Mediterranean lemon groves and vineyards of the south gradually shading to Teutonic schnitzel and beer on the north end)—can make for a great 1- or 2-day break from Italy's sightseeing carnival.

DON'T LEAVE MILAN & THE LAKE DISTRICT WITHOUT . . .

PAYING HOMAGE TO DA VINCI AND MICHELAN- GELO You'll find *The Last Supper* in Milan's Santa Maria delle Grazie and the *Pietà,* Michelangelo's last work, inside the medieval Castello Sforzesco.

CLIMBING TO THE ROOF OF THE MILAN DUOMO Wander amid the Gothic buttresses and statue-stopped spires for a citywide panorama.

SEEING THE BRERA AND AMBROSIANA PICTURE GALLERIES Tour these Milan museums packed with stunning works by such Old Masters as Raphael, Caravaggio, and Leonardo da Vinci.

TAKING A WINDOW-SHOPPING SPIN Walk past the high-end boutiques in Milan's Golden Rectangle, then go on a budget shopping spree through the stock shops and outlets of Corso Buenos Aires.

The town of Menaggio on Lake Como.

INDULGING IN THE NIGHTLIFE The converted warehouses along Milan's Navigli canals are always hopping after dark.

FERRYING BETWEEN LAKE MAGGIORE'S BORRO-MEAN ISLANDS There you can tour the palaces of one of Lombardy's last remaining Renaissance-era noble families and watch the peacocks wander their exotic gardens.

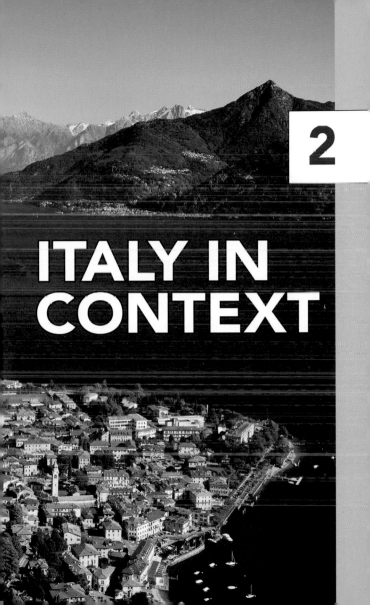

2

ITALY IN CONTEXT

As with any destination, a little background reading can help you to understand more. Many Italy stereotypes are accurate—children are fussed over wherever they go, food and soccer are like religion, the north–south divide is alive and well, bureaucracy is a frustrating feature of daily life. Some are wide of the mark—not every Italian you meet will be open and effusive. Occasionally they do taciturn pretty well, too.

The most important thing to remember is that, for a land so steeped in history—3 millennia and counting—Italy has only a short history *as a country.* In 2011 it celebrated its 150th birthday. Prior to 1861, the map of the peninsula was in constant flux. War, alliance, invasion, and disputed successions caused that map to change color as often as a chameleon crossing a field of wildflowers. Republics, mini-monarchies, client states, Papal states, and city-states, as well as Islamic emirates, colonies, dukedoms, and Christian theocracies, roll onto and out of the pages of Italian history with regularity. In some regions, you'll hear languages and dialects other than Italian. It's part of an identity that is often more regional than it is national.

This confusing history explains why your Italian experience will differ wildly if you visit, say, Turin

PREVIOUS PAGE: **Lake Como.**

rather than Naples. (And why you should visit both, if you can.) The architecture is different; the food is different; the important historical figures are different, as are the local issues of the day. And the people are different: While the north–south schism is most often written about, cities as close together as Florence and Siena can feel very dissimilar. This chapter will help you understand why.

ITALY TODAY

The big Italian news for many travelers is the recent favorable movement in exchange rates. Last year's edition of this guide listed the US dollar/euro exchange rate at $1.37. At time of writing, it's $1.06. Everything in Italy just became 22% cheaper for visitors from across the Atlantic. (The Canadian dollar has moved less dramatically, but still in the right direction—from $1.51 to $1.33.) So, congratulations: You picked a good time to visit.

Many Italians have not been so lucky. One reason for the euro's plunge is a stubbornly slow European recovery from the global financial crisis—known here as the *Crisi*. It had a disastrous effect on Italy's economy, causing the deepest recession since World War II. Public debt had grown to alarming levels—as high as 1,900 billion euros—and for more than a decade economic growth has been slow. As a result, 2011 and 2012 saw Italy pitched into the center of a European banking crisis, which almost brought about the collapse of the euro. By 2015, many Italians were beginning to see light at the end of their dark economic tunnel—a little, at least.

Populism has become a feature of national politics. A party led by comedian Beppe Grillo—the *MoVimento 5 Stelle* (Five Star Movement)—polled around a quarter of the vote in 2013 elections. By early 2014, in the postelectoral shakedown, former Florence mayor Matteo Renzi became Italy's youngest prime minister—at 39 years of age—heading a coalition of the center-left led by his Democratic Party (PD). Among his first significant acts was to name a governing cabinet made up of equal numbers of men and women, a ratio unprecedented in Italy. Opinion polling through mid-2015 showed Italians still favoring Renzi's reformism over rivals' policies.

Italy's population is aging, and a youth vacuum is being filled by immigrants, especially those from Eastern Europe, notably Romania (whose language is similar to Italian) and Albania, as well as from North Africa. Italy doesn't have the colonial experience of Britain and France, or the "melting pot" history of the New World; tensions were inevitable, and discrimination is a daily fact of life for many minorities. Change is coming—in 2013, Cécile Kyenge became Italy's first black government minister, and black footballer Mario Balotelli is one of the country's biggest sports stars. But it is coming too slowly for some.

A "brain drain" continues to push young Italians to seek opportunities abroad. The problem is especially bad in rural communities and on the islands, where the old maxim, "it's not what you know, it's who you know," applies more strongly than ever in these straitened times. By 2015, however, indicators suggested the worst of Italy's economic turmoil might be behind it. From top to toe, highlands to islands, fingers

cuisine **IN PIEDMONT & LOMBARDY**

Italians know how to cook—just ask one. But be sure to leave plenty of time: Once an Italian starts talking food, it's a while before they pause for breath. Italy doesn't really have a unified national cuisine; it's more a loose grouping of regional cuisines that share a few staples, notably pasta, bread, tomatoes, and pig meat cured in many ways. Probably the most famous dish of **Piedmont** and **Lombardy** is *cotoletta alla milanese* (veal dipped in egg and breadcrumbs and fried in olive oil)—the Germans call it Wienerschnitzel. *Osso buco* is another Lombard classic: shin of veal cooked in a ragout sauce. Turin's iconic dish is *bagna càuda*—literally "hot bath" in the Piedmontese language, a sauce made with olive oil, garlic, butter, and anchovies, into which you dip raw vegetables. Piedmont is also the spiritual home of *risotto*, particularly the town of Vercelli, which is surrounded by rice paddies.

are firmly crossed that the good times are coming round again.

THE MAKING OF ITALY
Prehistory to the Rise of Rome

Of all the early inhabitants of Italy, the most extensive legacy was left by the **Etruscans.** No one knows exactly where they came from, and the inscriptions that they left behind (often on graves in necropoli) are of little help—the Etruscan language has never been fully deciphered by scholars. Whatever their origins, within 2 centuries of appearing on the peninsula around 800 B.C., they had subjugated the lands now known as Tuscany (to which they left their name) and Campania, along with the **Villanovan** tribes that lived there.

From their base at **Rome,** the Latins remained free until they too were conquered by the Etruscans around 600 B.C. The new overlords introduced gold tableware and jewelry, bronze urns and terracotta statuary, and the art and culture of Greece and Asia Minor. They also made Rome the governmental seat of Latium. "Roma" is an Etruscan name, and the ancient kings of Rome had Etruscan names: Numa, Ancus, and even Romulus.

The Etruscans ruled until the **Roman Revolt** around 510 B.C., and by 250 B.C. the Romans and their allies had vanquished or assimilated the Etruscans, wiping out their language and religion. However, many of the former rulers' manners and beliefs remained, and became integral to what we now understand as "Roman culture."

Meanwhile, the **Greeks**—who predated both the Etruscans and the Romans—had built powerful colonial outposts in the south, notably in Naples, founded as Greek "Neapolis."

The Roman Republic: ca. 510–27 B.C.

After the Roman Republic was established around 510 B.C., the Romans continued to increase their power by conquering neighboring communities in the highlands and forming alliances with other Latins in the lowlands. They gave to their allies, and then to conquered peoples, partial or complete Roman citizenship, with the obligation of military service. Citizen colonies were set up as settlements of Roman farmers

Etruscan bronze of a she-wolf suckling twin brothers Romulus and Remus.

or military veterans, including both **Florence** and **Siena.**

The stern Roman Republic was characterized by a belief in the gods, the necessity of learning from the past, the strength of the family, education through reading and performing public service, and most importantly, obedience. The all-powerful Senate presided as Rome defeated rival powers one after the other and came to rule the Mediterranean. The Punic Wars with **Carthage** (in modern-day Tunisia) in the 3rd century B.C. presented a temporary stumbling block, as Carthaginian general **Hannibal** (247–182 B.C.) conducted a devastating campaign across the Italian peninsula, crossing the Alps with his elephants and winning bloody battles by the shore of **Lago Trasimeno,** in Umbria, and at Cannae, in Puglia. In the end, however, Rome prevailed.

No figure was more towering during the late Republic, or more instrumental in its transformation into the Empire, than **Julius Caesar,** the charismatic conqueror of Gaul—"the wife of every husband and the husband of every wife." After defeating the last resistance of the Pompeians in 45 B.C., he came to Rome and was made dictator and consul for 10 years.

Ancient Roman ruins on the Capitoline Hill.

Conspirators, led by Marcus Junius Brutus, stabbed him to death at the Theater of Pompey on March 15, 44 B.C., the "Ides of March." The site (at Largo di Torre Argentina) is best known these days as the home to a feral cat colony.

The conspirators' motivation was to restore the power of the Republic and topple dictatorship. But they failed: **Mark Antony,** a Roman general, assumed control. He made peace with Caesar's willed successor, **Octavian,** and, after the Treaty of Brundisium which dissolved the Republic, found himself married to Octavian's sister, Octavia. This marriage, however, didn't prevent him from also marrying Cleopatra in 36 B.C. The furious Octavian gathered western legions and defeated Antony at the **Battle of Actium** on September 2, 31 B.C. Cleopatra fled to Egypt, followed by Antony, who committed suicide in disgrace a year later. Cleopatra, unable to seduce his successor and thus retain her rule of Egypt, followed suit with the help of an asp. The permanent end of the Republic was nigh.

The Roman Empire in Its Pomp: 27 B.C.–A.D. 395

Born Gaius Octavius in 63 B.C., and later known as Octavian, **Augustus** became the first Roman emperor in 27 B.C. and reigned until A.D. 14. His autocratic reign ushered in the *Pax Romana,* 2 centuries of peace.

By now, Rome ruled the entire Mediterranean world, either directly or indirectly, because all political, commercial, and cultural pathways led straight to Rome, the sprawling city set on seven hills: the Capitoline, Palatine, Aventine, Caelian, Esquiline, Quirinal, and Viminal. It was in this period that **Virgil** wrote his best-loved epic poem, "The Aeneid," which supplied a grandiose founding myth for the great city and empire. Also in this prosperous era, **Ovid** composed his erotic poetry and **Horace** wrote his "Odes."

The emperors brought Rome to new heights. But without the checks and balances formerly provided by the Senate and legislatures, success led to corruption. These centuries witnessed a steady decay in the ideals and traditions on which the Empire had been founded. The army became a fifth column of unruly mercenaries, and for every good emperor (Augustus, Claudius, Trajan, Vespasian, and Hadrian, to name a few) there were several cruel, debased, or incompetent tyrants (Caligula, Nero, Caracalla, and many others).

After Augustus died (by poison, perhaps), his widow, **Livia**—a shrewd operator who had divorced her first husband to marry Augustus—set up her son, **Tiberius,** as ruler through intrigues and poisonings. A series of murders and purges ensued, and Tiberius, who ruled during Pontius Pilate's trial and crucifixion of Christ, was eventually murdered in his late '70s. Murder was so common that a short time later, **Domitian** (ruled A.D. 81–96) became so obsessed with the possibility of assassination that he had the walls of his palace covered in mica so that he could see behind him at all times. (He was killed anyway.)

Excesses ruled the day—at least, if you believe surviving tracts written by contemporary chroniclers infused with all kinds of bias: **Caligula** supposedly committed incest with his sister, Drusilla, appointed his horse to the Senate, lavished money on egotistical projects, and proclaimed himself a god. Caligula's successor, his uncle **Claudius,** was poisoned by his final wife—his niece Agrippina—to secure the succession of **Nero,** her son by a previous marriage. Nero's thanks were to later murder not only his mother but also his wife (Claudius's daughter) and his rival, Claudius's son. The disgraceful Nero, an enthusiastic persecutor of Christians, committed suicide with the cry, "What an artist I destroy!"

By the 3rd century A.D., corruption had become so prevalent that there were 23 emperors in 73 years. Few, however, were as twisted as **Caracalla** who, to secure control, had his brother Geta slashed to pieces while Geta was in the arms of his mother, former empress Julia Domna.

Constantine the Great became emperor in A.D. 306, and in 330, he made Constantinople (or Byzantium) the new capital of the Empire, moving the administrative functions away from Rome altogether, partly because the menace of possible barbarian attacks in the west had increased. Constantine was the first

ALL ABOUT vino

Italy is the largest **wine**-producing country in the world; as far back as 800 B.C. the Etruscans were vintners. However, it wasn't until 1965 that laws were enacted to guarantee consistency in winemaking. Quality wines are labeled **"DOC"** (Denominazione di Origine Controllata). If you see **"DOCG"** on a label (the "G" means *garantita*), that denotes an even better quality wine region. **"IGT"** (Indicazione Geografica Tipica) indicates a more general wine zone—for example, "Umbria"—but still with some quality control.

Piedmont: The finest reds in Italy probably hail from the vineclad slopes of Piedmont, particularly those made from the late-ripening **Nebbiolo** grape in the Langhe hills south of Alba. The big names—with big flavors and big price tags—are **Barbaresco** (brilliant ruby red with a delicate flavor) and **Barolo** (also brilliant ruby red, and gaining finesse when it mellows into a velvety old age).

Christian emperor, allegedly converting after he saw the "True Cross" in a dream, accompanied by the words: In this sign shall you conquer. He defeated rival emperor Maxentius and his followers at the **Battle of the Milivan Bridge** (A.D. 312), a victory that's remembered by Rome's triumphal **Arco di Costantino.** Constantine ended the persecution of Christians with the **Edict of Milan** (A.D. 313).

It was during the Imperial period that Rome flourished in architecture, advancing in size and majesty far beyond earlier cities built by the Greeks. **Classical orders** were simplified into types of column capitals: **Doric** (a plain capital), **Ionic** (a capital with a scroll), and **Corinthian** (a capital with flowering acanthus leaves). Much of this advance in building prowess was due to the discovery of a form of concrete and the fine-tuning of the arch, which was used with a logic, rhythm, and ease never before seen.

The Fall of the Empire Through the "Dark Ages"

The Eastern and Western sections of the Roman Empire split in A.D. 395, leaving the Italian peninsula without the support it had once received from east of the Adriatic. When the **Goths** moved toward Rome in the early 5th century, citizens in the provinces, who had grown to hate the bureaucracy set up by **Emperor Diocletian,** welcomed the invaders. And then the pillage began.

Rome was first sacked by **Alaric I,** king of the Visigoths, in 410. The populace made no attempt to defend the city, other than trying vainly to buy him off (a tactic that had worked 3 years earlier); most people fled into the hills. The feeble Western emperor **Honorius** hid out in **Ravenna** the entire time, which from 402 he had made the new capital of the Western Roman Empire.

More than 40 troubled years passed. Then **Attila the Hun** invaded Italy to besiege Rome. Attila was dissuaded from attacking, thanks largely to a peace mission headed by Pope Leo I in 452. Yet relief was short-lived: In 455, **Gaiseric,** king of the **Vandals,** carried out a 2-week sack that was unparalleled in its savagery. The empire of the West lasted for only another 20 years; finally, in 476, the sacks and chaos ended the once-mighty city, and Rome itself was left to the

A Growing Taste for Beer

Italy will always be known, and adored, for its wine. But one gastronomic trend to watch out for as you travel is the growth in popularity of artisanal beer, especially among the young. Although supermarket shelves are still stacked with mainstream brands Peroni and Moretti, smaller stores and bars increasingly offer craft micro-brews (known as *birre artigianali*). Italy had fewer than 50 breweries in 2000. That figure was well over 400 by 2015, and rising fast. You'll even find quality beers on the hallowed shelves of the occasional wine vendor.

popes, though it was ruled nominally from Ravenna by an Exarch from Byzantium (aka Constantinople).

Although little of the detailed history of Italy in the post-Roman period is known—and few buildings survive—it's certain that the spread of **Christianity** was gradually creating a new society. The religion was probably founded in Rome about a decade after the death of Jesus, and gradually gained strength despite early (and enthusiastic) persecution by the Romans.

The Middle Ages: 9th Century to the 14th Century

A ravaged Rome entered the Middle Ages, its once-proud people scattered in rustic exile. A modest population lived in the swamps of the **Campus Martius.** The seven hills—now without water because the aqueducts were cut—stood abandoned and crumbling.

The Pope turned toward Europe, where he found a powerful ally in **Charlemagne,** king of the Franks. In 800, Pope Leo III crowned him emperor. Although Charlemagne pledged allegiance to the church and looked to Rome and its pope as the final arbiter in most religious and cultural affairs, he launched northwestern Europe on a course toward bitter opposition to the meddling of the papacy in temporal affairs.

The successor to Charlemagne's empire was a political entity known as the **Holy Roman Empire** (962–1806). The new Empire defined the end of the Dark Ages but ushered in a long period of bloody warfare. Magyars from Hungary invaded northeastern Lombardy and, in turn, were defeated by an increasingly powerful **Venice.** This was the great era of Venetian preeminence in the eastern Mediterranean; it defeated naval rival **Genoa** in the 1380 Battle of Chioggia; great buildings like the **Doge's Palace** were built; its merchants reigned over most of the eastern Mediterranean, and presided over a republic that lasted for a millennium. The Lion of St. Mark—symbol of the city's dominion—can be seen as far afield as **Bergamo** (p. 82), close to Milan.

Rome during the Middle Ages was a quaint backwater. Narrow lanes with overhanging buildings filled many areas that had once been showcases of imperial power. The forums, mercantile exchanges, temples, and theaters of the Imperial era slowly disintegrated. As the seat of the Roman Catholic Church, the state was almost completely controlled by priests, and began an aggressive expansion of church influence and acquisitions. The result was an endless series of power struggles. Between 1378 and 1417, competing popes—one in Rome, another **"antipope"** in Avignon—made simultaneous claims to the legacy of St. Peter.

In the mid–14th century, the **Black Death** ravaged Europe, killing perhaps a third of Italy's population. Despite such setbacks, Italian **city-states** grew wealthy from Crusade booty, trade, and banking.

The medieval period marks the beginning of building in stone on a mass scale. Flourishing from A.D. 800 to 1300, **Romanesque** architecture took its inspiration and rounded arches from ancient Rome. Architects built large churches with wide aisles to accommodate the masses.

Romanesque **sculpture** was fluid but still far from naturalistic. Often wonderfully childlike in its narrative simplicity, the work frequently mixes biblical scenes with the myths and motifs of local pagan traditions that were being incorporated into medieval Christianity. The exterior of Parma's **Baptistery** sports a

Milan's Duomo, a classic Gothic cathedral.

**The A-List of Italian Novels
Available in English**

- Alessandro Manzoni, *The Betrothed* (1827)
- Alberto Moravia, *The Conformist* (1951)
- Giuseppe Tomasi di Lampedusa, *The Leopard* (1958)
- Elsa Morante, *History: A Novel* (1974)
- Italo Calvino, *If on a Winter's Night a Traveler* (1979)
- Umberto Eco, *Foucault's Pendulum* (1988)
- Niccolo Ammaniti, *I'm Not Scared* (2001)

---

series of Romanesque friezes by Benedetto Antelami (1150–1230).

As the appeal of Romanesque and the Byzantine faded, the **Gothic** style flourished from the 13th to the 15th centuries. In architecture, the Gothic was characterized by flying buttresses, pointed arches, and delicate stained-glass windows. These engineering developments freed architecture from the heavy, thick walls of the Romanesque and allowed ceilings to soar, walls to thin, and windows to proliferate.

Although the Gothic age continued to be religious, many secular buildings also arose, including palaces designed to show off the prestige of various ruling families. Milan's **Duomo** (p. 38) is one of Europe's great Gothic cathedrals.

The medieval period also saw the birth of literature in the Italian language—which itself was a written version of the **Tuscan dialect,** primarily because the great writers of the age were Tuscans. Florentine **Dante Alighieri** wrote his *Divine Comedy* in the 1310s. Boccaccio's *Decameron*—kind of a Florentine *Canterbury Tales*—appeared in the 1350s.

Renaissance & Baroque Italy

The story of Italy from the dawn of the Renaissance in the early 15th century to the "Age of Enlightenment" in the 17th and 18th centuries is as fascinating.

Milan was a glorious Renaissance capital, particularly under the Sforza dynasty and Ludovico "Il Moro" (1452–1508), patron of Leonardo da Vinci.

This era is best remembered because of its art, and around 1400 the most significant power in Italy was the city where the Renaissance began: **Florence**. Slowly but surely, the **Medici** family rose to become the most powerful of the city's ruling oligarchy, gradually usurping the powers of the guilds and the republicans. They reformed law and commerce, expanded the city's power by taking control of neighbors such as **Pisa,** and also sparked a "renaissance," a rebirth, in painting, sculpture, and architecture. Christopher Hibbert's *The Rise and Fall of the House of Medici* (2001) is the most readable account of the era.

Under the patronage of the Medici (as well as other powerful Florentine families), innovative young painters and sculptors went in pursuit of a greater degree of expressiveness and naturalism.

Ghiberti's Baptistery Doors, a Renaissance masterpiece in Florence.

Next followed the brief period that's become known as the **High Renaissance:** The epitome of the Renaissance man, Florentine **Leonardo da Vinci** (1452–1519), painted his "Last Supper," now in Milan's **Santa Maria delle Grazie** (p. 50), and an "Annunciation" (1481), now hanging in Florence's **Uffizi** alongside countless Renaissance masterpieces from such great painters as Paolo Uccello, Sandro Botticelli, Piero della Francesca, and others. **Raphael** (1483–1520) produced a sublime body of work in 37 short years.

Skilled in sculpture, painting, and architecture, **Michelangelo** (1475–1564) and his career marked the apogee of the Renaissance. His giant "David" at the **Galleria dell'Accademia** in Florence is the world's most famous statue, and the **Sistine Chapel** frescoes have lured millions to the **Vatican Museums** in Rome.

In time, the High Renaissance stagnated, paving the way for the **baroque.** Stuccoes, sculptures, and paintings were carefully designed to complement each other—and the space itself—to create a unified whole. The baroque movement's spiritual home was Rome, and its towering figure was **Gian Lorenzo Bernini** (1598–1680), the greatest baroque sculptor, a fantastic architect, and a more-than-decent painter as well.

In painting, the baroque mixed a kind of super-realism based on using everyday people as models and an exaggerated use of light and dark—a technique called *chiaroscuro*—with compositional complexity and explosions of dynamic fury, movement, and color. The period produced many fine artists, notably **Caravaggio** (1571–1610). Among his masterpieces are the

"St. Matthew" (1599) cycle in Rome's **San Luigi dei Francesi** and "The Acts of Mercy" in **Pio Monte della Misericordia,** Naples.

Frothy, ornate, and chaotic, **rococo** art was the baroque gone awry—and had few serious proponents in Italy. **Giambattista Tiepolo** (1696–1770) was arguably the best of the rococo painters, and specialized in ceiling frescoes and canvases with cloud-filled heavens of light. He worked extensively in Venice and the northeast.

At Last, a United Italy: The 1800s

By the 1800s, the glories of the Renaissance were a fading memory. From Turin to Naples, chunks of Italy had changed hands many, many times—between the Austrians, the Spanish, and the French, among autocratic thugs and enlightened princes, between the noble and the merchant classes. The 19th century witnessed the final collapse of many of the Renaissance city-states. The last of the Medici, Gian Gastone, had died in 1737, leaving Tuscany in the hands of Lorraine and Habsburg princes.

French emperor **Napoleon** brought an end to a millennium of Republic in **Venice** In 1797, and installed puppet or client rulers across the Italian peninsula. During the **Congress of Vienna** (1814–15), which followed Napoleon's defeat by an alliance of the British, Prussians, and Dutch, Italy was once again divided.

Political unrest became a fact of Italian life, some of it spurred by the industrialization of the north and some by the encouragement of insurrectionaries like **Giuseppe Mazzini** (1805–72). Europe's year of

Giuseppe Garibaldi.

revolutions, **1848,** rocked Italy, too, with violent risings in Lombardy and Sicily. After decades of political machinations and intrigue, and thanks to the efforts of statesman **Camillo Cavour** (1810–61) and rebel general **Giuseppe Garibaldi** (1807–82), the Kingdom of Italy was proclaimed in 1861 and **Victor Emmanuel (Vittorio Emanuele) II** of Savoy became its first monarch. The kingdom's first capital was **Turin** (1861–65), seat of the victorious Piedmontese, followed by **Florence** (1865–71).

The establishment of the kingdom, however, didn't signal a complete unification of Italy because Latium (including Rome) was still under papal control and Venetia was held by Austria. This was partially resolved in 1866, when Venetia joined the rest of Italy after the **Seven Weeks' War** between Austria and Prussia. In 1871, Rome became the capital of the newly formed country, after the city was retaken on September 20, 1870. Present-day **Via XX Settembre** is the very street up which patriots advanced after breaching the city gates. The **Risorgimento**—the "resurgence," Italian unification—was complete.

The 20th Century: Two World Wars & One Duce

In 1915, Italy entered **World War I** on the side of the Allies. Italy joined Britain, Russia, and France to help defeat Germany and the traditional enemy to the north, now the Austro-Hungarian Empire, and so to "reclaim" Trentino and Trieste. (Mark Thompson's *The White War* tells the story of Italy's catastrophic campaign.) In the aftermath of war and carnage, Italians further suffered with rising unemployment and horrendous inflation. As in Germany, this deep political crisis led to the emergence of a dictator.

On October 28, 1922, **Benito Mussolini,** who had started his Fascist Party in 1919, knew the country was ripe for change. He gathered 30,000 Black Shirts for his **March on Rome.** Inflation was soaring and workers had just called a general strike, so rather than recognizing a state under siege, **King Victor Emmanuel III** (1900–46) proclaimed Mussolini as

La Scala opera house.

the new government leader. In 1929, Il Duce—a moniker Mussolini began using from 1925—defined the divisions between the Italian government and the Pope by signing the Lateran Treaty, which granted political, territorial, and fiscal autonomy to the microstate of **Vatican City.** During the Spanish Civil War (1936–39), Mussolini's support of Franco's Fascists, who had staged a coup against the elected government of Spain, helped seal the Axis alliance between Italy and Nazi Germany. Italy was inexorably and disastrously sucked into **World War II.**

The era's towering figure in music was **Giacomo Puccini** (1858–1924); his operas *Tosca* (1900) and *Madame Butterfly* (1904) still pack houses worldwide.

After defeat in World War II, Italy's people voted for the establishment of the First Republic— overwhelmingly so in northern and central Italy, which counterbalanced a southern majority in favor of keeping the monarchy. Italy quickly succeeded in rebuilding its economy, in part because of U.S. aid under the **Marshall Plan** (1948–52). By the 1960s, as a member of the European Economic Community (founded by the **Treaty of Rome** in 1957), Italy had become one of the world's leading industrialized nations, and prominent in the manufacture of automobiles and office equipment. Fiat (from Turin), Ferrari (from Emilia-Romagna), and Olivetti (from northern Piedmont) were known around the world.

The country was plagued, however, by economic inequality between the industrially prosperous north and the depressed south, and during the late 1970s and early 1980s, it was rocked by domestic terrorism:

These were the so-called **Anni di Piombo (Years of Lead),** during which extremists of the left and right bombed and assassinated with impunity. Conspiracy theories became the Italian staple diet; everyone from the state to shady Masonic lodges to the CIA was accused of involvement in what became in effect an undeclared civil war. The most notorious incidents were the kidnap and murder of Prime Minister **Aldo Moro** in 1978 and the **Bologna station bombing,** which killed 85 in 1980. You'll find a succinct account of these murky years in Tobias Jones's *The Dark Heart of Italy* (2003).

The postwar Italian **film industry** became respected for its innovative directors. **Federico Fellini** (1920–93) burst onto the scene with his highly individual style, beginning with *La Strada* (1954) and going on to such classics as *The City of Women* (1980). His *La Dolce Vita* (1961) defined an era in Rome.

In the early 1990s, many of the country's leading politicians were accused of corruption. These scandals uncovered as a result of the judiciary's **Mani Pulite (Clean Hands)** investigations—often dubbed **Tangentopoli** ("Bribesville")—provoked a constitutional crisis, ushering in the **Second Republic** in 1992.

Other resonant events in recent Italian history have centered on its religion. As much of the world watched and prayed, **Pope John Paul II** died in April 2005, at the age of 84, ending a reign of 26 years. A Vatican doctrinal hard-liner next took the papal throne as **Pope Benedict XVI.** He was succeeded by the surprisingly liberal **Pope Francis** in 2013, after Benedict became the first pope to resign since the 1400s.

WHEN TO GO

The best months for traveling in Italy are from **April to June** and **mid-September to October**—temperatures are usually comfortable, rural colors are richer, and the crowds aren't too intense (except around Easter). From **July through early September** the country's holiday spots teem with visitors. **Easter, May,** and **June** usually see the highest hotel prices in Rome and Florence.

August is the worst month in most places: Not only does it get uncomfortably hot, muggy, and crowded, but seemingly the entire country goes on vacation, at least from August 15 onward—and many Italians take off the entire month. Many family-run hotels, restaurants, and shops are closed (except at the spas, beaches, and islands, where most Italians head). Paradoxically, you will have many urban places almost to yourself if you visit in August. Turin and Milan, in particular, can seem virtual ghost towns, and hotels there (and often in Florence and Rome) are heavily discounted. Just be aware that many fashionable restaurants and nightspots are closed for the whole month.

From **late October to Easter,** many attractions operate on shorter (sometimes *much* shorter) winter hours, and some hotels are closed for renovation or redecoration, though that is less likely if you are visiting the cities. Many family-run restaurants take a week or two off sometime between **November and February;** spa and beach destinations become padlocked ghost towns.

Weather

It's warm all over Italy in summer; it can be very hot in the south, and almost anywhere inland—landlocked cities on the plains of Veneto and Emilia-Romagna, and in Tuscany, can feel stifling during a July or August hot spell. The higher temperatures (measured in Italy in degrees Celsius) usually begin everywhere in May, often lasting until sometime in October. Winters in the north of Italy are cold, with rain and snow. A biting wind whistles over the mountains into Milan, Turin, and Venice.

The rainiest months pretty much everywhere are usually October and November.

Public Holidays

Offices, government buildings (though not usually tourist offices), and shops in Italy are generally closed on: January 1 (*Capodanno,* or New Year); January 6 (*La Befana,* or Epiphany); Easter Sunday (*Pasqua*); Easter Monday (*Pasquetta*); April 25 (Liberation Day); May 1 (*Festa del Lavoro,* or Labor Day); June 2 (*Festa*

Bellagio on Lake Como.

della Repubblica, or Republic Day); August 15 (*Ferragosto,* or the Assumption of the Virgin); November 1 (All Saints' Day); December 8 (*L'Immacolata,* or the Immaculate Conception); December 25 (*Natale,* Christmas Day); December 26 (*Santo Stefano,* or St. Stephen's Day). You'll also often find businesses closed for the annual daylong celebration dedicated to the local saint (for example, on January 31 in San Gimignano, Tuscany).

EXPLORING MILAN

3

Milan—or Milano, as the Italians say it—is elegant, chaotic, and utterly beguiling. Traffic chokes the streets, and it can be bitterly cold in winter and stiflingly hot in summer, yet its architecture is majestic and the robust Northern Italian cuisine warming. It's a world-class stop on the international fashion stage, the banking capital of Italy, a wealthy city of glamorous people and stylish shopping streets.

And Milan has history. As well as the Roman ruins, the soaring Duomo and its majestic piazza, the galleries are stuffed with priceless artworks, and there are

552km (342 miles) NW of Rome, 288km (179 miles) NW of Florence, 257km (159 miles W of Venice) 140km (87 miles) NE of Turin, 142km (88 miles) N of Genoa

ancient churches, medieval castles, Renaissance palaces, and amazing contemporary architecture to admire.

In 2015, Milan hosted the 6-month-long **Expo Milano 2015,** focused on the theme "Feeding the Planet. Energy for Life," in a suburban area northwest of the *centro storico.* Massive changes were made to the city in preparation, including a new cluster of buildings constructed in the CityLife district, featuring innovative towers by international archistars Arata Isozaki, Daniel Libeskind, and Zaha Hadid.

PREVIOUS PAGE: **Milan's famous Duomo.**

Exploring Milan

Remember to dress modestly when visiting Milan's churches; no short shorts for either sex, women must have their shoulders covered, and skirts must be below the knee. The dress code at the Duomo is particularly strict.

Castello Sforzesco ★ MUSEUM   Although it has lived many lives under several different occupiers and been restored many times, this fortified castle is the masterpiece of Milan's two most powerful medieval and Renaissance dynasties, the Visconti and the Sforza. The Visconti built the castle (and the Duomo) in the 14th century before the Sforzas married into their clan, eclipsed their power, and took their castle in the 1450s, turning it into one of the most gracious palaces of the Renaissance. Sforza *capo* Ludovico il Moro and his wife Beatrice d'Este also helped transform Milan into one of Italy's great centers of the Renaissance by commissioning works by Bramante, Michelangelo, and Leonardo da Vinci.

The castle's most recent restoration was at the hands of architect Luca Beltrami at the end of the 19th century; it opened as a museum in 1905. Today it contains a dozen museums and archives, known collectively as the Musei del Castello Sforzesco. Many of the Sforza treasures are on view in the miles of rooms that surround the castle's labyrinthine courtyards, stairways, and corridors. They include a *pinacoteca* with works by Bellini and Correggio plus Spanish Mannerists Ribera and Ricci. The extensive holdings of the Museo d'Arte Antica include the final work of 89-year-old Michelangelo; his evocative, unfinished "Pietà Rondanini" is found in the Sala degli Scarlioni.

On the second floor, the highlight of the decorative arts collection is the "Cassone del Tre Duchi," a

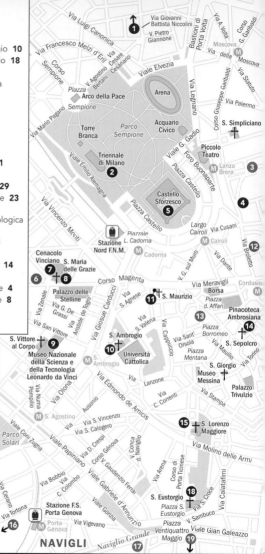

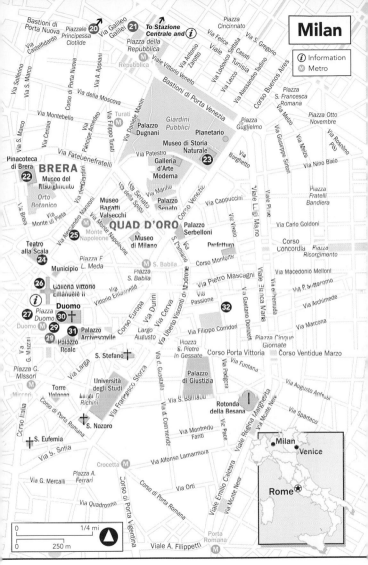

chest commissioned by the Sforzas in 1494 and decorated with images of the dukes in full military regalia. The main attractions of the applied art galleries are the exquisite Trivulzio Tapestries by Bramantino in the Sala della Balla.

Piazza Castello. www.milanocastello.it. ✆ **02-8846-3700.** Castle courtyards: Free admission. Daily 7am–6pm (summer until 7pm). Musei del Castello Sforzesco: Admission 5€ (free Tues 2–5:30pm; Wed–Thurs and Sat–Sun 4:30–5:30pm). Tues–Sun 9am–5:30pm (last admission 30 min. before closing). Metro: Cairoli.

Duomo di Milano ★★★ CHURCH Although there has been a church here since at least A.D. 355, building started on the present exterior of Milan's magnificent Gothic Duomo in the late 14th century, to a design by Gian Galeazzo Visconti (1351–1402). Marble slabs for the facade were transported from quarries bordering Lake Maggiore into the city along the Navigli canals. It was consecrated in 1418, but the enormous dome wasn't added until the 16th century and the

Aerial view of Milan.

Duomo was not deemed complete until 1965, when the mammoth cast-bronze doors were finally finished.

Today the cathedral's facade has emerged sparkling from the scaffolding that had engulfed it since 2009 (although restoration work continues down its southern flank). Once again it dominates the vast, traffic-free **Piazza del Duomo** (see p. 46). Able to accommodate 40,000 people, it is one of the world's largest churches (St. Peter's in Rome takes the record), with an embellished triangular facade encrusted with flying buttresses plus around 2,300 statues and gargoyles. Pinnacles bristle on the domed roof, topped by a 5m (16-ft.) gilded figure of the Virgin Mary, known as **La Madonnina** and regarded as Milan's lucky mascot.

The interior of the Duomo is surprisingly subdued and serene, despite the hordes of tourists who pour in daily. The floors are of complex patterned marble reflecting patterns of sunlight as it streams through jewel-like stained-glass windows. Rows of 52 marble columns divide the space into five cavernous aisles, and the side chapels are dotted with Renaissance and Mannerist tombs.

In the crypt, the **Baptistero di San Giovanni alle Fonti** reveals the remains of the octagonal 4th-century foundations of the original church (ticket included in admission to the Museo del Duomo), which is almost certainly where Sant'Ambrogio, patron saint and Bishop of Milan in A.D. 374, christened the great missionary St. Augustine. Pride of place in the Treasury goes to the ornate **gilded tomb of Carlo Borromeo** (see p. 120), Archbishop of Milan and leader of the Counter-Reformation, who died in 1584.

Piazza del Duomo. www.duomomilano.it. ✆ **02-7202-2656.** Free admission. Daily 7am–7pm. Metro: Duomo.

Shoppers at the Galleria Vittoria Emanuele II.

Galleria Vittorio Emanuele II ★★ SHOPPING MALL   Milan's most elegant shopping arcade links the Piazza del Duomo with Piazza della Scala, site of the famous opera house. The gallery, which was spruced up during the preparations for Expo 2015, is entered through an enormous Neo-Classical triumphal archway leading to a shopping mall blessed with ornate marble flooring and a massive octagonal glass dome. Inside, the arcade is lined with genteel grand cafes such as Biffi and Il Savini, where the local elite gather to dine after a night at the opera. The designer stores here currently include Gucci, Versace, Prada, Louis Vuitton, and Swarovski.

Galleria Vittorio Emanuele II was the master-piece of Bolognese architect Giuseppe Mengoni, who designed it in the 1870s to mark the unification of Italy under King Vittorio Emanuele II; note how the mosaic and fresco decorations incorporate patriotic symbols and coats of arms of various Italian cities. Unfortunately Mengoni never saw his magnus opus flourishing, as he died in a fall from scaffolding the day before it opened in 1878. Today giggling crowds gather under the soaring dome to spin around on one heel on the private parts of a little mosaic bull in the floor, a legendary good-luck ritual. At press time, the city was considering creating a panoramic terrace inside the galleria to offer visitors a birds-eye view of what is considered to be the "living room" of the Milanesi.

Piazza del Duomo. Open 24 hours. Metro: Duomo.

Museo Archeologico ★★ MUSEUM   Milan's beautifully curated archaeology museum is no dusty old relic but a vibrant, fascinating exhibition, a series of airy galleries housed among the cloisters, towers, and court-yards of the 8th-century convent of Monastero Mag-giore of San Maurizio. Subdivided into eight themed exhibitions, including Ancient Milanese, Greek, and Etruscan displays, the museum is built around the remains of a villa and a section of the 4th-century Roman walls that once fortified Milan. Roman Milan was known as Mediolanum; this area of the city is particu-larly rich in ruins dating back to the time when it was capital of the Western Roman Empire. Most of the trea-sures exhibited were excavated locally.

The museum now incorporates a glimpse inside a third century defense tower, with traces of medieval frescoes on its rounded walls; these portray Jesus showing his stigmata to St. Francis. Highlights of the collections include the 1st-century B.C. **mosaic pave-ment** unearthed nearby in 1913; the stunning, gleam-ing 4th-century **Trivulzio Diattreta Cup,** made of

spying ON MILAN

Take the trip up to the Duomo (www.duomomilano.it) roof for spine-tingling views across the rooftops of Milan and, on a clear day, to the Alps beyond. Elevators (12€) are found on the church's northeast corner, while stairs to the top (7€) are on the north flank. As well as the panorama, you can get up close to the Gothic pinnacles, saintly statues, and flying buttresses, as well as the spire-top gold statue of **"La Madonnina"** (the little Madonna), the city's beloved good-luck charm. The elevator is open daily 9am–6:30pm (last ticket sold at 6pm).

Other sneaky viewpoints over the Duomo include the food market on the top floor of classy department store **La Rinascente** and the posh **Restaurant Giacomo Arengario** (see p. 74) at the **Museo del Novecento** (see p. 43). To look down on Parco Sempione and the crowds in the Triennale Design Museum, take the elevator up Torre Branca near the north end of the park (Viale Alemagna, open mid-May to mid-Sept, hours vary).

the finest hand-blown glass; and the busts of various emperors from Caesar onwards.

Corso Magenta 15. www.comune.milano.it. ✆ **02-8844-5208.** Admission 5€ adults, 3€ reduced-price admission. Free Tues after 2pm. Tues–Sun 9am–5:30pm. Metro: Cadorna.

Museo del Duomo ★★★ MUSEUM The new jewel in the crown of Milan's museums opened in November 2013 on the ground floor of the Palazzo Reale. Enter on the left of the courtyard, to the right of the Duomo as you look at the facade. Incredible treasures from the Duomo are displayed here in an imaginatively curated exhibition, leading visitors on a chronological journey through the life of both Milan and its cathedral. Highlights among the carved cherubs, angels, and Renaissance Madonnas include a room full of startling gargoyles, ethereal 15th-century stained-glass works, scale wooden models of the cathedral, and the original supporting structure of **"La Madonnina"** (see p. 42), who has adorned the Duomo rooftop since 1774. Perhaps the standout piece is **"Jesus and the Moneylenders"** by Tintoretto, rediscovered by happy accident in the Duomo sacristy after World War II.

Piazza del Duomo 12. http://museo.duomomilano.it. © **02-7202-2656.** Admission 6€, 4€ under 26 and seniors. Tues–Sun 10am–6pm. Metro: Duomo.

Museo del Novecento ★ MUSEUM Opened in 2010, the futuristic building of the city's museum of 20th-century art forms a modern wing of the Palazzo Reale. You reach it via a circular concrete passageway, which winds up to the museum entrance on the third floor. The undisputed star of the collection is Giuseppe Pellizza da Volpedo's painting **"The Fourth Estate"** (1901), which is free for all to admire in the passageway outside the museum. Otherwise the collection showcases Italian modern art from Futurist to Arte Povera, making the case that Italy's contribution to the world of art did not halt with the Renaissance. There are some brilliant bursts of genius in the exhibition, such as the magnificent **"Philosopher's Troubles"** (1926) by Giorgio de Chirico and the moving **"Thirst"** (1934) by sculptor Arturo Martini, so stick with it. Temporary exhibitions in the Palazzo Reale are accessible by the exit from the museum, but be warned, the signage is confusing.

Palazzo dell'Argenario, Piazza del Duomo 12. www.museodel novecento.org. © **02-7634-0809.** Admission 10€ adults, 8€ students and seniors. Mon 2:30–7:30pm, Tues–Sun 9:30am–7:30pm (Thurs, Sat until 10:30pm). Metro: Duomo.

Museo Nazionale della Scienza e della Tecnologica Leonardo da Vinci ★★ MUSEUM

The Leonardo Lab at the Museo Nazionale della Scienza e della Tecnologica Leonardo da Vinci.

This cavernous monolith's main building is constructed around the twin courtyards and three floors of the former monastery of San Vittore Olivetan, plus three modern additions and outdoor spaces. While recent renovations have made the exhibits more interactive and fun, the floor plan is still immensely confusing, and it's a big museum; pick up a brochure so you don't miss the highlights. These include a clutch of Leonardo's anatomical drawings and not-so-batty designs for flying machines on the top floor, a display of 20th-century technology that will shock teenagers for how rudimentary it is, and a mini-submarine ride (book in advance: ✆ 02-4855-5330; Tues and Thurs after 1:30pm; 10€). The Air and Water Building has lots of full-size airplanes and boats to explore; there's a railway track full of locomotives, and interactive labs for kids to play around with basic experiments.

Via San Vittore 21. www.museoscienza.org. ✆ 02-485-551. Admission 10€ adults, 7.50€ under 25, 4.50€ seniors. Guided tour of activities in English 65€ for 1 hour. Tues–Sun 9:30am–5pm. Metro: Sant'Ambrogio.

Museo Poldi Pezzoli ★★ ART GALLERY This wonderfully eclectic art collection was the life's work of aristocrat Gian Giacomo Poldi Pezzoli, who donated his lifetime's investment in artwork and decorative arts to the city of Milan in 1879; it is now elegantly displayed in his luxurious former *palazzo*. The ornate rooms of the ground floor feature Oriental rugs, weapons, ancient armor, and rare books. Up the carved marble stairs the riches continue, through extravagant rooms hung with family portraits, displaying hand-blown Murano glass and dainty Limoges china. Scenes from *The Divine Comedy* are featured in stained glass,

cruising **THE CANALS**

Take Metro Line 2 to Porta Genova to explore Milan's Navigli area (*navigli* means canals), the perfect spot for a relaxed drink, people-watching, and a late-night supper. Crowded and full of life, these few streets are refreshingly casual in ambience after the dressy obsession of the city center—it's one of the few places in Milan where you will see punks, hippies, and Goths, or find vintage stores.

Building started in the late 13th century on the Navigli canals, designed initially to transport marble slabs from quarries along Lake Maggiore (see p. 114) into the city to build the Duomo. The Naviglio Grande was Europe's first major canal and is one of the great engineering marvels of the medieval era. Used to import food, commodities, and trade goods, the canals were crucial to Milan's infrastructure until the 1970s, when road transport won out and several waterways were filled in. Take a boat tour of the canals to peek into Milan's industrial heritage; **Navigli Lombardi** (www.naviglilombardi.it; ✆ **02-6679131**) runs daily tours.

and fine gilded pistols sit side by side with precious jewelry.

The stars of this wonderful show are the intricate **Armillary Sphere,** crafted by Flemish clockmaker Gualterus Arsenius in 1568 to illustrate contemporary theories of planetary movement, and the **Renaissance paintings** by Botticelli and Piero della Francesca in the Golden Room. And still the collection grows: Recent acquisitions include a set of gold-and-ivory netsuke and a curiously intimate set of lacy bonnets for babies dating from the 18th century.

Via Manzoni 12. www.museopoldipezzoli.it. ℓ **02-794-889.** Admission 10€ adults, 7€ seniors and students 11–18, free under 10. Audioguides 5€. Wed–Mon 10am–6pm, closed Tues. Metro: Montenapoleone.

Piazza del Duomo ★★ PIAZZA The Piazza del Duomo has been the beating heart of Milan since the city was settled by the Romans in 220 B.C. and known as Mediolanum. This vast traffic-free piazza sees local life passing to and fro daily, added to by the bustle of tourists peering up at the majestic Duomo while dodging pigeons and street sellers pushing cheap souvenirs. From here a tangle of narrow streets branch off in all directions through the city's *centro storico* (historic center). The square took on its present form following the Unification

Milan's Piazza del Duomo.

of Italy in 1861, when the medieval buildings were replaced by splendid neoclassical buildings designed by Giuseppe Mengoni (1829–1877), also architect of the **Galleria Vittorio Emanuele II** (see p. 40) and the sculptor of the equestrian statue of Vittorio Emanuele II in the middle of the square.

The piazza is home to the superb **Museo del Duomo** (see p. 42), temporary art exhibitions in the **Palazzo Reale** (www.comune.milano.it; ✆ 02-0202), and the 20th-century Italian art in the **Museo del Novecento** (see p. 43).

Metro: Duomo.

Pinacoteca Ambrosiana ★★ ART GALLERY

Founded in 1609 to display the private collections of the pious Cardinal of Milan Federico Borromeo, this gallery is housed in the world's second-oldest public library (after the Bodleian in Oxford, U.K.). While the emphasis is on Italian art from the 15th to early 20th centuries, some Dutch work is also exhibited.

Despite the confusing layout encompassing courtyards, passageways, stairwells, and any number of tiny exhibition rooms, the gallery is well worth visiting for four outstanding works of art: the fine portrait of **"The Musician"** by Leonardo da Vinci (1490); the cartoon for **"The School of Athens"** by Raphael (1510); Caravaggio's cute **"Basket with Fruit,"** painted around 1599; and Titian's **"Adoration of the Magi"** (ca. 1550).

Leonardo's original "Codex Atlanticus" is in the Biblioteca Ambrosiana next door along with other rare manuscripts; drawings from the "Codex" can be seen in the Sacristy of Bramante in Santa Maria della Grazie.

Piazza Pio XI. www.ambrosiana.eu. ✆ **02-806-921.** Admission to pinacoteca and sacristy 20€ adults, 15€ children 13 and under. Pinacoteca only 10€. Tues–Sun 10am–6pm. Metro: Duomo or Cordusio.

MILAN'S time-travel CHURCHES

Milan has been an important center of Christianity since Emperor Constantine sanctioned the faith in a.d. 313. There are more than 100 churches in Milan and, like the Duomo, many of them lie on pagan foundations. In these, layer upon layer of history can be stripped back to their early remains.

Two such churches are on Corso di Porta Ticinese. **The Basilica di San Lorenzo Maggiore** was built in the 4th century, using rubble removed from the amphitheater nearby, at the same time as the 16 Corinthian columns standing outside. The church now has a 16th-century facade, but inside, fragments of the original building survive: The octagonal, white-washed Cappella di Sant'Aquilino retains pieces of the 4th-century gold mosaic that once covered all the walls, and to the right of this stairs lead down to the foundations of the first basilica.

A step further along Corso di Porta Ticinese, the **Basilica di Sant'Eustorgio** has undergone many facelifts. The foundations of the original 4th-century church

Pinacoteca di Brera ★★★ ART GALLERY Milan's, and indeed Lombardy's, premier art collection resides over an art school in a 17th-century Jesuit college, wrapped around a two-story arcaded courtyard. This peerless collection romps in a circular tour through Italian art from medieval to Surrealism in 38 roughly chronological rooms. Along the way there are splendid Renaissance altarpieces, Venetian School and Baroque paintings, gloomy Mannerist works, and, thanks to recent donations, the odd piece by Picasso and Umberto Boccioni to enjoy.

are behind the altar in the basilica, although the present Neo-Romanesque facade dates from 1865. The ornate Cappella Portinari dates from the 15th century, built as a memorial to St. Peter.

In Piazza Sant'Ambrogio you'll find the sublime Lombard Romanesque **Basilica di Sant'Ambrogio.** Built over a Roman cemetery, the church was extensively remodeled from the 8th to 11th centuries, and it is here that the remains of Milan's patron saint, Ambrogio, are housed. The glittering mosaics in the apse and wall frescoes in the side chapels show scenes from the life of the saint, and a great gold altar constructed in the 9th century holds his remains.

The Baroque church of **Santa Maria del Carmine** in Brera was built over the remains of a Romanesque basilica and partly remodeled in 1400; most of its present incarnation dates from 1447. The Gothic-Lombard facade was added in 1880, making the church a true mishmash of styles.

Although the collection is not immense, it is of exquisite quality; just some of the breathtaking highlights include Piero della Francesca's sublime **Montefeltro Altarpiece** (1474); the ethereal **"Cristo Morto"** by Andrea Mantegna (1480); Caravaggio's superb, if mournful, 17th-century **"Supper at Emmaus"** (1601); and Raphael's **"Marriage of the Virgin"** (1504), which was beautifully restored in the glass-walled, temperature-controlled restoration rooms that are open to the public.

Of the secular work in the gallery, standout pieces include Francesco Hayez's **"The Kiss"** (1859) and artist Giovanni Fattori's pastoral scenes, which lead the way for the Macchiaioli School of Italian Impressionists from the late 19th century. Bringing the collection all the more up to date are donations including a clutch of works by Italian playboy artist Amedeo Modigliani and the sculptor Marino Marini.

Via Brera 28. www.brera.beniculturali.it. ℂ 02-722-632-64. Admission 10€ adults, 7€ seniors and students under 18. Audioguide 5€. Tues–Sun 8:30am–7:15pm. Metro: Lanza.

Santa Maria delle Grazie ★★ CHURCH The delightful Lombard Renaissance church of Santa Maria delle Grazie is often ignored in the mad scramble to see Leonardo da Vinci's world-renowned "Last Supper" in the *cenacolo* (refectory) of the Dominican convent attached to the church. Started in 1465–1482 by Gothic architect Guiniforte Solari (ca. 1429–1481), the church was subsequently enlarged when the Sforza duke Ludovico il Moro decided to make it his family mausoleum. He commissioned Leonardo da Vinci to paint the "Last Supper," and asked Donato Bramante, the leading light of the Lombard Renaissance who also had a hand in the design of St Peter's in Rome, to add the terracotta-and-cream arcaded apse in 1492. Inside the church itself, a clash of styles is evident between Solari's heavily frescoed Gothic nave and Bramante's airy, somber apse.

Piazza Santa Maria delle Grazie. www.grazieop.it. No phone. Free admission. Mon–Sat 7am–noon, 3–7:15pm; Sun 7:30am–12:30pm, 3:30pm–9pm. Metro: Cadorna or Conciliazione.

Santa Maria delle Grazie, Il Cenacolo Vinciano ★★★ CHURCH Milan's greatest art treasure is also one of the most famous on earth, largely thanks to Dan Brown's blockbuster novel *The Da Vinci Code*.

Painted for Milanese ruler Ludovico il Moro by Leonardo da Vinci between 1495 and 1497, "The Last Supper" adorns the back wall of the refectory in the Dominican convent attached to the church of Santa Maria delle Grazie. Leonardo's masterpiece depicts Christ revealing that one of his disciples will soon betray him; horror and disbelief are etched on every face, while Jesus remains calm and resigned. As we look at the fresco, Judas sits to the left of Jesus, leaning away from him with the bag of silver clearly visible in his right hand. Is it Mary Magdalene sitting between him and Jesus? Wherever you stand on the controversy, there is no doubt that "The Last Supper"

Seeing "The Last Supper"

Unsurprisingly, Leonardo's "The Last Supper" is on almost every tourist's itinerary of Milan. And with only 30 people allowed in to the Cenacolo Vinciano at a time, it is a challenge to get a ticket if you don't book well in advance. Try the official website first, www.cenacolo vinciano.net, or call ℭ **02-9280-0360** (tickets are 6.50€ from the website, plus a 1.50€ booking fee) **3 months** before you are due to visit. Tickets are sold online for visits 3 months ahead. Present your e-tickets at the booking office outside the

Cenacolo in Piazza Santa Maria delle Grazie at least 20 minutes before your allotted time slot. And remember that the Cenacolo is not in the church of Santa Maria delle Grazie itself, but in the refectory behind it, with a separate entrance of its own.

If you've missed the opportunity to snag a ticket in advance, many tour companies guarantee admission to "The Last Supper" as part of their guided tours of the city, which range from 40€ to 70€ (see "Organized Tours," p. 53).

is one of the world's most poignant and beautiful works of art.

Due to da Vinci experimenting with his painting technique and applying tempera straight on to the walls of the refectory, his sublime fresco began to deteriorate virtually on completion. It suffered several ham-fisted restoration attempts in the 18th and 19th centuries and survived target practice by Napoleon's troops, not to mention a period exposed to the open air after Allied bombing in WWII. The latest cleanup of the fresco was completed in 1999, and while the colors are muted, they are thought to resemble Leonardo's original fresco. The famous fresco is now climate-controlled for preservation, and groups of only 30 at a time are allowed in to view it, in pre-allocated periods of 15 minutes.

Piazza Santa Maria delle Grazie 2. www.cenacolovinciano.net, © **02-9280-0360.** Admission 6.50€ adults, 3.25€ ages 4–17 and seniors. 1.50€ booking fee applies to all tickets. Tues–Sun 8:15am–7pm. Metro: Cadorna or Conciliazione.

Triennale di Milano ★★★ MUSEUM Opened in 2007, this sleek, white temple of cool is dedicated to contemporary design, and as you'd expect in this city of stylistas, it's busy day and night. Located at the north end of Parco Sempione just by the Torre Branca, it features on-trend temporary exhibits, anything from black-and-white photography to retrospectives on Italian design icons. On the second floor an internal bridge, designed by Michele de Lucchi from sheets of bamboo, leads from the exhibition spaces into the Triennale Design Museum (separate entry fee), which has oft-changed displays of modern Italian design classics, well signposted in English. The Agora Theater puts on innovative shows and the bookstore is *the*

The Triennale Museum.

place to pick up beautifully produced full-color coffee-table tomes. A lovely spot with views over Parco Sempione, the DesignCafé and Restaurant is the venue of choice on Sundays for smart Milanese and their immaculately turned-out offspring.

Viale Alemagna 6. www.triennale.it. ✆ **02-724-341.** Admission to Design Museum 8€ adults, 6€ students 25 and under, seniors 65 and over. Temporary exhibits range from free to 0€. Tues–Wed and Fri–Sun 10:30am–8:30pm; Thurs 10:30am–11pm. Metro: Cadorna or Cairoli.

Organized Tours

Among the scores of companies offering guided tours of Milan and Lombardy, here are three of the best. **Viator** (www.viator.com; U.S. ✆ **702-648-5873**) offers private guided tours of Milan with hotel pick-ups as well as sightseeing tours by Segway, plus jaunts out to the lakes Como and Maggiore. **Zani Viaggi** (www.zaniviaggi.it; ✆ **02-867-131**) leads specialist tours to the revered turf of San Siro Stadium (see below) and the shopping outlets of northern Lombardy, while **Local Milan Tours** (www.localmilantours.com; U.S. ✆ **866/663-7017**) can organize trips around La Scala (see p. 81) and day trips as far afield as Venice.

Outdoor Activities

Milan is a densely populated urban sprawl where green space is rare and precious. The largest park is the 47-hectare (116-acre) expanse of **Parco Sempione** behind Castello Sforzesco. It is the lungs of the city, the favorite place of well-heeled Milanese to walk their dogs along shady pathways sheltered by giant chestnuts; it is here that lovers come to moon around the ornamental lakes designed in English Romantic fashion by Emilio Alemagna in the early 1800s. The **Giardini Pubblici** on Bastioni di Porta Venezia is another haven, a firm favorite with families at the weekend for its little fair. Joggers circuit the park, and in winter there's ice-skating on the ornamental ponds. **Parco Solari** and **Gardaland Waterpark** (see p. 56) have swimming pools, and **Idroscalo** (see p. 57) at Linate offers every outdoor activity from sailing and swimming to climbing or tennis. The **Lombardy lakes** all offer the chance for watersports, cycling, and hiking. For sports fanatics, San Siro Stadium (www.sansiro.net; ✆ **02-4879-8201**) and **Monza F1 racetrack** (see p. 58) are open for tours.

Especially for Kids

Despite being world-renowned as a hub of high finance, fashion, and design, Milan is after all an Italian city and all Italians dote on children. The city's rather formal facade belies its many family-friendly attractions, museums, *gelaterie*, and play parks, and everywhere you go, your *bambini* will be worshipped, hugged, and multilaterally adored.

Where to start? Chief among attractions that all kids will love is the ride up to the **Duomo rooftop** (see p. 42) for views across the red rooftops of the city to the Alps. The basement level of the **Museo Nazionale della Scienza e della Tecnologica Leonardo da Vinci** (see p. 44) is stuffed full of fun, interactive activities for kids. Children ages 4 to 11 can be distracted by the play area Sforzinda in the **Castello Sforzesco's** (see p. 35) 14th-century dungeons while parents explore the decorative arts. A picnic lunch and a run around in the adjoining **Parco Sempione** is a welcome respite from cultural overload.

The new **Museo dei Bambini** (Via Enrico Besana 12; www.muba.it; ✆ **02-4398-0402**) doesn't have a permanent collection, but offers creative and educational workshops for children ages 2 and up. Opening times and cost of workshops vary, but tend to run around 10 euros. The museum also has a café and a large garden around the historic circular structure, the late-Baroque Rotonda della Besana, which has been everything from a cemetery for the poor to a stable to a home for the chronically ill.

Another great green public space is the **Giardini Pubblici** (see p. 54) Here there are playgrounds, roundabouts, and a little electric train that chugs around the park. The Corso Venezia side of the park is home to the **Museo di Storia Naturale** (www.comune.milano.it; ✆ **02-8846-3337;** Tues–Sun 9am–5:30pm; admission 5€), where you can take the kids to see the dinosaur skeletons and the carcasses of massive bugs. As for swimming pools in the city, there's

out and about AT THE THEME PARKS

Italy's version of Disneyland, **Gardaland**, is located a couple of hours from Milan in Castlenuovo del Garda (see p. 130), but there are plenty of options closer to the city. Located on the far western outskirts of town, the Milan offshoot of Gardaland, **Gardaland Waterpark** (Via Gaetano Airaghi 61; www.gardalandwaterpark.it; ✆ **02-4820-0134**), has splashy water slides, fun rides, and picnic areas. It typically opens at the end of May and stays open until the end of August. To get there, take the red subway line (direction Rho Fieramilano) to the Lotto stop, then bus 423 (direction Settimo Milanese) to Via Airaghi. The park is open daily 10am to 7pm. Admission is free but you pay by activity; an all-day ticket costs 18€ adults and 12€ for children under 12 (on Sundays, adult tickets are 20€). Enter after 2:30 p.m. for slightly reduced tickets. Swimming pools are 8€ on the weekend, and parking is 2€.

About 30 minutes northeast of Milan in the direction of Bergamo, the **Leolandia** amusement park (Via Vittorio Veneto 52, Capriate San Gervasio; www.leolandia.it) has rides and games for kids of all ages, as well as the delightful Minitalia, a replica of all of the major cities and monuments in Italy. More compact and manageable than the main Gardaland, it may be better suited to smaller children, with features such as Peppa Pig World, opened in 2015 as a draw for the toddler set. Full-price tickets purchased at the park cost 31.50€, but can be had for half that online. Children up to 89 cm (about 3 feet) enter free. Leolandia opens in April and stays open through Halloween (in fact, the park has special Halloween celebrations, which is unusual—Halloween isn't widely celebrated in Italy). In early spring and fall, it's open only weekends, in June and July it's open Wednesday to Sunday, and it's open daily in August. The Z301 bus from Milan to Bergamo, managed by **Nord Est Trasporti** (www.nordesttrasporti.it; ✆ **800-905-150**), stops near Leolandia, at Capriate San Gervasio.

Cars race around the Autodromo Nazionale Monza.

a municipal swimming pool in **Parco Solari** (Via Montevideo 20).

Near the Linate airport, just east of the city center, the **Idroscalo** park (Via Circonvallazione Idroscalo 29, Segrate; www.idroscalo.info; no phone) features a manmade lake that was originally created for seaplanes to land. This area has now been turned into a park open daily (summer 7am–9pm, winter 7am–5pm) and offers loads of sporting activities from sailing and swimming to climbing and ping-pong. There are also a couple of clubs and restaurants in the park where one can have a lounge-y, leisurely brunch on Sundays (try Le Jardin Au Bord du Lac, for example: www.lejardin auborddulac.com, Via Circonvallazione 51). Take the ATM Line 73 bus to Linate airport, then ATM Line 183 or 923 to Idroscalo. At night it is best to take a taxi as public transportation runs less frequently.

Most restaurants will happily rustle up a child's portion of pasta and tomato sauce, and if all else fails, it's usually easy to bribe any child with a visit to one of Milan's delicious ice cream shops; try **Biancolatte** (Via Turati 30; ✆ **02-6208-6177**) for dark-chocolate ice-cream cakes and **Rinomata Gelateria** (Ripa di Porta Ticinese 1; ✆ **02-5811-3877**) in Navigli for the most traditional ice-cream cones in town.

Outlying Attractions

Autodromo Nazionale Monza ★★ RACING CIRCUIT Sprawled along the River Lambro in Lombardy, and 15km (10¼ miles) northeast of Milan, Monza is an appealing city with a central core reminiscent of a mini-Milan; it has a majestic early-Gothic Duomo and photogenic piazzas backed by lots of greenery. Sadly, the centro storico is usually bypassed in favor of the 10km (6.2-mile) Formula One racetrack that is the epicenter of car-mad Italy's hopes and dreams. The home of the Italian Grand Prix since 1922, Monza track is now open to all aspiring speed demons that fancy being a racing driver for the day. Race training sessions are held daily, with half-hour slots available for would-be champions to try out their skills on the track. Rallies, endurance races, and special events take place all year around while the Italian Formula One Grand Prix is held in September in front of hundreds of thousands of fans. Check the website for tickets and event details.

Via Vedano 5, Monza. www.monzanet.it. ✆ **039-2482-239.** Accessible by train (15 min.) from Centrale and Garibaldi stations.

Certosa di Pavia.

Certosa di Pavia ★★★ CHURCH Located a few miles north of the town of Pavia, this awesome Carthusian monastery is well worth a day trip. It was originally commissioned in 1396 as a mausoleum for Milan's ruling family the Viscontis, but after the Viscontis' dynastic downfall, the Sforza family took over, refurbishing the monastery according to their exorbitant tastes. The result is a highly intricate Renaissance façade, the swansong of master 15th-century architect Giovanni Antonio Amadeo, who also worked on the **Basilica di Santa Maria Maggiore in Bergamo** (see p. 86). The monastery contains the ornate tomb (but not the bodies) of Ludovico del Moro and his wife Beatrice, who together shaped the Milanese Renaissance. A tour takes in the peaceful cloisters, monks' cells, and refectory, but the highlight of this lovely place is the decorative church, its swaths of frescoes, the *pietra dura* altar, and the massive **mausoleum** of Gian Galeazzo Visconti.

Via Del Monumento 4, Certosa di Pavia. www.comune.pv.it/certosadipavia. © **0382-925-613.** Admission and guided tours by donation. Open Tues–Sun. May–Aug 9–11:30am, 2:30–6pm; Mar–Apr, Sept 9–11:30am, 2:30–5:30pm; Oct 9–11:30am, 2:30–5pm; Nov–Feb 9–11:30am, 2:30–4pm. Accessible by train from Milan Stazione Rogoredo (Metro Line 3) to Certosa (3.60€), then a 15-minute walk.

Outlying Attractions

EXPLORING MILAN

MILAN
ESSENTIALS

4

ilan's increasing popularity has meant that travelers do better booking hotels well in advance, and considering advance reservations for restaurants, as well. This chapter gives you our recommendations on both those topics, plus all you need to know about getting to and around the city.

4 | Essentials

GETTING THERE

BY PLANE   Both of Milan's major airports are operated by **SEA** (www.seamilano.eu; ✆ **02-232-323**). **Milan Malpensa,** 45km (28 miles) northwest of the center, is Milan's major international airport. The **Malpensa Express** train (www.malpensaexpress.it; ✆ **02-7249-4949**), costs 12€ and leaves from Terminal 1 with a 30-minute run half-hourly to Cadorna train station, or hourly to Stazione Centrale (45 min). Buses also run directly to Stazione Centrale, a 50-minute journey, with 5 departures per hour, for 10€ per single journey or 16€ round-trip; they're operated by **Malpensa Shuttle** (www.malpensashuttle.it; ✆ **02-5858-3185)** or **Autostradale** (www.autostradale.it; ✆ **02-5858-7304**). By taxi, the trip into town costs a wallet-stripping 90€ and takes about 50 minutes. It's the only option after midnight.

   Milan Linate, 7km (4.5 miles) east of the center, handles European and domestic flights. **Air Bus**

PREVIOUS PAGE: **Shoppers at the Galleria Vittorio Emanuele II.**

Milan's Shut-Down Mondays

Don't get caught out when planning your trip to Milan; bear in mind that almost the whole city closes down for at least half a day on Monday, though this tradition is slowly being phased out. Most popular attractions, churches, and state-owned museums, with the exception of the **Duomo** (see p. 38) and the **Museo Poldi Pezzoli** (which has Tuesday off instead), are closed all day Monday. About half the stores are closed Monday mornings, with most reopening around 3:30 to 7:30pm.

(www.atm-mi.it; © **02-48-607-607**) makes the 25-minute trip by bus every 30 minutes between 6am and midnight from Linate to Milan's Stazione Centrale for 5€. City bus no. 73 leaves every 10 minutes for the San Babila Metro stop downtown (1.50€) and takes 25 minutes. The express no. X73 is faster and departs every 20 minutes between 7am and 8pm, with tickets costing 1.50€. The trip into town by taxi costs roughly 20€.

Malpensa Shuttle buses also connect Malpensa and Linate airports with five daily services between 9:30am and 6:20pm. The trip takes 90 minutes and costs 13€ (roundtrip 26€).

BY TRAIN Milan is one of Europe's busiest rail hubs. Trains travel every half-hour to Bergamo (1 hr.), Mantua (2 hr.), and Turin (1 hr. by the AV high-speed train). **Stazione Centrale** is a half-hour walk northeast of the center, with easy connections to Piazza del Duomo by Metro, tram, and bus. The station stop on the Metro is Centrale F.S. Multilingual automatic ticket machines accept cash and credit cards but *not* debit cards. You may need to validate your ticket in the machines at the beginning of the track as you get on your train, especially if you don't have an e-ticket.

Stazione Centrale is Milan's major station, but trains also serve **Cadorna** (Como and Malpensa airport), and **Porta Garibaldi** (Lecco and the north). All these stations are on the green Metro Linea 2.

BY BUS Long-distance buses are useful for reaching the ski resorts in Valle d'Aosta. Most bus services depart from Lampugnano bus terminal (Metro: Lampugnano) although some originate in Piazza Castello (Metro: Cairoli). **Autostradale** (www.autostradale.it; ☏ **02-5858-7304**) operates most of the bus lines and has ticket offices in front of Castello Sforzesco on Piazza Castello, open daily 9am to 6pm, and in front of the Duomo in Passageway 2 next to the TIM mobile phone store, open weekdays 8:30am to 6pm and weekends 9am to 4pm. **Savda** (www.savda.it; **0165-367-011**) runs five daily buses (more in the winter) between Milan Lampugnano and Aosta (2½ hr.; 17€) or Courmayeur (3½ hr.; 19.50€).

BY CAR The A1 autostrada links Milan with Florence (3 hr.) and Rome (6 hr.), while the A4 connects Milan with Verona (2 hr.) and Venice (2½ hr.) to the east and Turin (1 hr.) to the west.

GETTING AROUND

BY TRAIN Milan's most famous sights are within walking distance of each other, but the public transport system, an integrated system of **Metro, trams, and buses,** run by **ATM** (www.atm.it; ☏ **02-48-607-607**), is a cheap and effective alternative to walking. The Metro closes at midnight (Sat at 1am), but buses and trams run all night. Metro stations are well signposted; trains are speedy, clean, safe, and frequent—they run every couple of minutes during the day and

Milan's trams.

about every 5 minutes after 9pm. Tickets for 90 minutes of travel on Metro, trams, or buses cost 1.50€. A 24-hour unlimited travel ticket is a better value at 4.50€ and a 2-day ticket goes for 8.25€. Tickets are available at newsstands and Metro stations (all machines have English-language options; the 24-hr. ticket option is listed under "Urban"). Stamp your ticket when you board a bus or tram—there is a 35€ fine (more if not paid on the spot) if you don't. For more information, visit the ATM information offices in the Duomo Metro, Stazione Centrale, and Cadorna, all open Monday to Saturday, 7:45am to 8pm.

Lines 1 (red, with stops at Cairoli for Castello Sforzesco and Duomo for Galleria Vittorio Emanuele II and the Duomo) and 3 (yellow, with a stop at Via Montenapoleone) are the most useful for sightseeing.

BY CAR   Driving and parking in Milan are not experiences to relish. First of all, you'll have to pay the Area C congestion charge of 5€ to enter the *centro storico* Monday to Friday, 7:30am to 7:30pm. On top of that, the one-way system is complicated, some streets are reserved for public transport only, and there are many pedestrianized areas. Hotels will make parking arrangements for guests—take advantage of that.

BY TAXI   Taxis are located in major *piazze* and by major Metro stops. There is a taxi stand in Piazza del Duomo and outside Castello Sforzesco; a journey between the two will cost around 7€. Hotel reception staff can call a taxi for you; otherwise, a reliable company is **Taxiblu** at ✆ **02-4040.** Meters start at 3.30€ and prices increase by 1.09€ per kilometer. Expect surcharges for waiting time, luggage, late-night travel, and Sunday journeys.

BY BIKE   With the streets of the *centro storico* largely pedestrianized, Milan is a good city for cycling, with a handy bike-sharing program, **BikeMi.** The tariff for the pass is typically convoluted: For 2.50€ a day or 6€ a week, you can buy a pass that allows 30 minutes of free travel. The next 2 hours are charged at 0.50€ per 30 minutes (or fraction of it) up until 2 hours, and thereafter your time is charged at 2€ per hour or fraction of it. Pick up one of the distinctive custard-yellow bikes at racks from outside Castello Sfozesco and the Duomo as well as at tram, bus, and metro stops. Buy your pass online (www.bikemi.com); at the **ATM Points** at Centrale, Cadorna, Garibaldi, and Duomo stations from 7:45am to 8pm; or by calling ✆ **02-48-607-607.**

ON FOOT   The attractions of the *centro storico* are all accessible on foot. From Piazza del Duomo, Via Montenapoleone is a 10-minute walk through Piazza della Scala and along Via Manzoni, and it is a 10-minute

---

Milano Discount Card

The **MilanoCard** (www.milano card.it) offers a great deal on Milan sightseeing at just 6.50€ for 24 hours or 13€ for 3 days. You get a lot for your buck, including free travel on all public transportation, discounts in some stores and restaurants, and reduced entry to more than 20 museums and galleries. Each card is valid for one adult and a child under 10—a brilliant value for the money.

walk to Castello Sforzesco. Santa Maria delle Grazie and "The Last Supper" are a 30-minute stroll from Piazza del Duomo.

VISITOR INFORMATION

The main **Azienda di Promozione Turistica (APT) tourist office** is in Galleria Vittorio Emanuele on the corner of Piazza della Scala (www.visitamilano.it; © **02-8845-5555**). It's open Monday to Friday 9am to 7pm, Saturday 9am to 6pm, and Sunday 10am to 6pm. There is an office in **Stazione Centrale** (© **02-7740-4318**), after the police command station and track 21, open Monday to Friday 9am to 6pm and Saturday and Sun from 9am to 1:30pm and 2pm to 6pm.

CITY LAYOUT

Milan developed as a series of circles radiating out from the central hub, Piazza del Duomo. Within the inner circle are most of the churches, museums, and shops of the *centro storico*. **Parco Sempione** and Leonardo's "The Last Supper" are to the west in the well-heeled neighborhood of Magenta. The slightly grungy cafe-filled districts of **Porta Ticinese** and **Navigli** lie directly south, with genteel **Brera** and its classy stores and restaurants slightly to the north. The **Quadrilatero d'Oro (Golden Quadrilateral)** is the mecca of Milanese fashion shoppers and is northeast of the Duomo, although **Via Tortona** near the Navigli is quickly developing as a funky shopping option. A burgeoning new **financial district** is growing between Porta Garibaldi and Centrale stations, while the towers of **CityLife** have taken over the old fairgrounds area (the new fairgrounds are located in Rho).

[FastFACTS] MILAN

ATMs/Banks

Banks with multilingual ATMs are all over the city center. Opening hours are roughly Monday to Friday 8:30am to 1:30pm and 3 to 4pm, with major branches opening Saturday morning for a couple of hours. Central branches may also stay open through lunch.

Business Opening Hours

Most stores in central Milan are open Tuesday to Saturday, 9:30am to 7:30pm, with a half-day Monday (3:30–7:30pm). Most shops close on Sundays and some still close for lunch between 12:30pm and 3:30pm.

Consulates

U.S. Consulate is at Via Princip-Amedeo 2/10 (*©* **02-290-351**), and is open Monday to Friday,

8:30am to noon for emergencies, otherwise by appointment (Metro: Turati). **Canadian Consulate** is at Piazza Cavour 3 (*©* **02-626-942-38**); it's open Monday to Friday from 9am to 1pm. Appointment recommended. (Metro: Turati). **British Consulate** is at Via San Paolo 7 (*©* **02-723-001**), open Monday to Friday from 9am to 5pm. (Metro: Duomo). **Australian Consulate,** at Via Borgogna 2 (*©* **02-776-741**), is open from Monday to Thursday 9am to 5pm and on Fridays from 9am to 4:15pm (Metro: San Babila). **New Zealand Consulate** is at Via Terraggio 17 (*©* **02-7217-0001**); office hours are Monday to Friday from 9am to 5pm (Metro: Cadorna).

Crime

For police emergencies, dial *©* **112** (a free call). There is a police station in Stazione Centrale but the **Questura** is the main station, just west of the Giardini Pubblici at Via Fatebenefratelli 11 (*©* **02-62-261;** Metro: Turati).

Dentists

Excellence Dental Network at Via Mauro Macchi 38 near Stazione Centrale (www.excellence dentalnetwork.com; *©* **02-7628-0498**) has English-speaking staff.

Doctors

Milan Medical Center at Via Angelo Mauri 3, near Cadorna station (www.milanmedical center.it; *©* **338-1651-324** for emergencies) has a multilingual staff.

Drugstores

Pharmacies rotate

24-hour shifts. Signs in most pharmacies post the schedule. The **Farmacia Stazione Centrale** (📞 **02-669-0735**) in Stazione Centrale is open 24 hours daily and the staff speaks English.

Emergencies All emergency numbers are free. Call 📞 **112** for a **general emergency**; this connects to the **Carabinieri,** who will transfer your call as needed; for the **police,** dial 📞 **113;** for a **medical emergency** or an ambulance, call 📞 **118;** for the **fire department,** call 📞 **115.**

Hospitals The **Ospedale Maggiore Policlinico**

(📞 **02-55-031**) is a 5-minute walk southeast of the Duomo at Via Francesco Sforza 35 (Metro: Duomo or Missori). Most of the medical personnel speak English.

Internet The free **Open Wi-Fi Milano** network has hundreds of hotspots all over the city, with Internet access for phones, tablets, and laptops. In addition, many Milanese hotels, bars, and cafes offer free Wi-Fi. Throughout the city, branches of the **Arnold Coffee** (www.arnoldcoffee. it) American-style coffee bars offer free Wi-Fi.

Post Office The main post office, **Poste e Telecommunicazioni,** is al Via Cordusio 4 (📞 **02-7248-2126;** Metro: Cordusio). It's open Monday to Friday 8am to 7pm and Saturday 8:30am to 1:50pm. The post office in Stazione Centrale is open Monday to Friday 8am to 5:30pm and Saturday from 8:15am to 3:30pm. Other branches are open Monday to Saturday 8:30am to 1:30pm.

Safety Milan is generally safe, although public parks and the area around Stazione Centrale are best avoided at night.

Where to Stay

Milan is northern Italy's biggest commercial center, big on banking and industry, and for years its hotels have tended to chase expense-account customers, often to the detriment of tourists and families. The winds of change are blowing, however. A recent wave of cozy, independent *locandas* and *albergos,* as well as design-conscious boutique hotels, have come along to complement the grand old institutions.

Note that prices are often higher during the week than on the weekend, and room rates really soar when the fashion crowd hits town (late Feb and late Sept).

EXPENSIVE

Hotel Principe di Savoia ★★

This lovely, grand Beaux Arts institution is now part of the Dorchester Collection, which has busily been collecting famous hotels in Europe and on the west coast of the U.S. There's still nowhere better for a truly luxurious stay in Milan than this five-star respite from the urban intensity, where every conceivable guest whim is swiftly addressed. Guests have access to serene gardens, a soothing top-floor spa, a quality restaurant, an elegant bar, and opulent, suitably swagged rooms and suites. Former guests include George Clooney, Madonna,

Junior Suite at the Hotel Principe di Savoia.

and the boys of One Direction, among others. Not surprisingly this luxury comes at a price, but for a bit of old-fashioned glamour, there's nowhere else like it.

Piazza Della Repubblica 17. www.dorchestercollection.com/en/milan/hotel-principe-di-savoia. © 02-623-01. 301 units. 250€–510€ double; 310€–4,700€ suite. Free parking valet service extra. Metro: Repubblica. **Amenities:** 1 restaurant; bar; concierge; room service; babysitting; spa; gym; indoor pool; Wi-Fi (free/high-speed service 9€ per day).

Milanosuites ★★★ Long considered one of the best-kept secrets in Milan, the former Antica Locanda dei Mercanti had a thorough facelift and re-emerged as the elegant, light-filled Milanosuites, set in a charming 18th-century townhouse tucked away in the appealing rabble of streets between the Castello Sforzesco and Piazza del Duomo. The number of guest rooms was reduced, making way for glamorous suites graced with parquet floors and simple white furnishings. All have living rooms and some have kitchenettes. Families can book a suite with two bedrooms.

Via San Tomaso 8. www.milanosuites.it. © 02-8909-6849. 5 units. 280€–320€ suite. Metro: Cordusio or Cairoli. **Amenities:** Concierge; room service; Wi-Fi (free).

nhow Milan ★★ A boutique hotel that is currently the darling of the fashion set, the nhow is part of a chain intent on providing stylish, well-priced accommodation, but somehow it feels a bit soulless. The sleek reception area sets the scene with an orange color scheme straight from the 1960s, only to be outdone by the lime-green furnishings in the minimalist bar, usually inhabited by gossiping models. Glass elevators whiz up to rooms decorated in white and slashes of bright color; the standard rooms are compact with walk-in showers. The fourth floor is the preserve of

The hipster lobby of the nHow Milan.

stylish, loft-style suites with views over Milan's burgeoning Zona Tortona fashion district. Porta Genova Metro station is close by.

Via Tortona 35. www.nhow-milan.com. ℓ **02-489-8861.** 246 units. 189€–289€ double; 419€–2,200€ suite. Rates include breakfast. Parking 24€ per day. Metro: Porto Genova. **Amenities:** Restaurant; bar; spa; gym; Wi-Fi (free).

MODERATE

Antica Locanda Leonardo ★★★ This lovely old-school *albergo* in snooty Corso Magenta looks inward on a surprisingly tranquil courtyard garden. It's like stepping into a family home; the rooms have been extensively revamped but still retain their wonderfully traditional feel, with heavy antique headboards and dressers, gilt mirrors, and elegant draperies. The bathrooms have also been dragged into the 21st century, but the cozy lounge and breakfast room remain delightfully of a former age. The pricier courtyard-facing rooms, most of which have tiny wrought-iron balconies, deflect the late-night noise on Corso Magenta.

Corso Magenta 78. www.anticalocandaleonardo.com. ℂ **02-4801-4197.** 16 units. 100€–320€ double (garden side are more expensive). Rates include breakfast. Parking 28€ per day. Metro: Concilliazione, Cardorna. **Amenities:** Concierge; Wi-Fi (free).

INEXPENSIVE

BioCity Hotel ★★★ This fab little *albergo* offers the best value for accommodation in Milan. It's all a budget hotel should be: small and pristine, with a miniscule bar and breakfast room and a tiny terrace out back—*and* it's eco-friendly. Guest rooms are stylish, with big bathrooms that would enhance a four-star hotel. The reception area manages to squeeze in a little lounge that's furnished with edgy pieces. Plus there's even a tiny shop selling organic goodies. Operated by genial, well-informed owners, the BioCity is a few minutes' walk from Stazione Centrale in an area kindly referred to as "up and coming." It's close to Metro Linea 3, which zips straight into the *centro storico.*

Via Edolo 18. www.biocityhotel.it. ℂ **02-6670-3595.** 17 units. 72€–90€ double. Rates include breakfast. Street parking free; covered parking 20€ per day. Metro: Sondrio. **Amenities:** Bar; Wi-Fi (free).

Where to Eat

There are thousands of eateries in Milan, from pizzerias to grand old cafes, gourmand Michelin-starred restaurants in highfalutin surroundings to corner bars with a great selection of *aperitivo*-time tapas, *gelaterie* to traditional *osterie.* Avoid the obvious tourist traps along Via Dante or indeed any place that has a menu showing photos of the dishes and you can't go far wrong.

Cocktail hour starts at around 6:30pm. Around that time, a tapaslike spread of olives, crudités, cold pasta dishes, rice, salads, salamis, and breads make its appearance in every city bar worth its salt. This is when the Milanese appear as if by magic, from shopping or work, to meet up for cocktails, a bitter Campari, or a glass of prosecco. By the time *aperitivo* hour is over, thoughts turn towards supper and the restaurants start to fill up. This phenomenon takes place all over Milan. Every night.

EXPENSIVE

Carlo e Camilla in Segheria ★★ MODERN ITALIAN   Celebrated chef Carlo Cracco's latest venture, in an old sawmill outside the *centro storico,* offers up an innovative new concept. The restaurant and cocktail bar has a sparse yet warm post-industrial feel with one long communal table for up to 65 people and large chandeliers hanging from the ceiling. Come for a truly unique cocktail from head mixologist Filippo Sisti (some say these are the best drinks in town) or stay for dinner with modern Italian food that is clean, fresh, and "not too cerebral." The menu features dishes like spaghetti with anchovies, lime, and coffee, or the salmon "cube" with a yogurt and lemongrass sauce.

Via G. Meda 24. www.carloecamillainsegheria.it. ℂ **02-837-3963.** Dishes range from 15€–25€. Mon–Sun. 6pm–2am. Metro: Romolo though Tram 3 from the Duomo gets you closer to the restaurant as it passes right outside.

Restaurant Giacomo Arengario ★★★ NORTHERN ITALIAN   Deserving of three stars just for its views of the Duomo, this super-hot spot is currently the number-one choice for smartly attired Milanese business lunchers and it's just as popular with tourists for the view. There's a smart little bar reminiscent of a Marrakesh casbah on acid where *aperitivi* are served early in the evening, but the real point here is to get seated by those plate-glass windows and gawk at the Duomo. The menu is a gourmet take on Milanese specialties; *fritto misto* comes fried in a lighter-than-light batter and is simply delicious accompanied by a spicy rocket salad, while the risotto comes perfectly prepared and slips down a treat with a glass of prosecco. There's a cover charge of 5€.

Via Guglielmo Marconi 1. www.giacomoarengario.com. ℰ 02-72-093-814. Main courses 18€–50€. Daily noon–midnight. Metro: Duomo.

MODERATE

Hostaria Borromei ★★ LOMBARDY This stalwart Milanese favorite with a delicious down-home vibe and hearty Lombardian gastronomy needs booking in advance for weekend dining, especially on the vineyard terrace for summer dining. The menu features

The patio of the Hostaria Borromei.

polenta, thick homemade noodle pastas, saffron-flavored risotto, the famed veal shank dish *osso bucco*, and plenty of seafood. Seasonal cheeses and traditional puddings such as *tiramisu* and *panna cotta* round off a warming dining experience in lively surroundings.

Via Borromei 4. www.hostariaborromei.com. ✆ **02-8645-3760.** Main courses 18€–44€. Mon–Fri 12:30–2:45pm and 7:30–10:45pm; Sat–Sun 7:30–10:45pm. Metro: Cordusio or Duomo.

Osteria il Kaimano ★★ NORTHERN ITAL-IAN   A good pick among the buzzing restaurants and bars of Brera, this casual, gently chaotic *osteria* is just the job for people-watching, Saturday lunchtime or a late-night dinner. The menu of pasta and pizza staples may not be vastly different from the other Brera dining options—**Sans Egal** (Vicolo Fiori 2; www.sansegal.it; ✆ 02-869-3096) and **Nabucco** (Via Fiori Chiari 10; www.nabucco.it; ✆ **02-860-663**) are also good choices—but here the atmosphere and service shine. Strong choices include the zucchini flowers stuffed with ricotta for starters (12€) and vast pizzas that continually pile out of the wood-burning oven. There's a little terrace on the street for summer eating, but in winter the smokers are all relocated here.

Via Fiori Chiari 20. ✆ **02-8050-2733.** Main courses 15€–40€. Daily noon–2:30pm, 6–11:30pm. Metro: Lanza Brera.

Pizzeria Tradizionale ★★ PIZZERIA   One of the busiest pizzerias in Milan is found down at the Navigli; it's a simple affair, with checked tablecloths. Tradizionale is always crammed with happy families devouring enormous crispy pizzas piled high with local salamis and mozzarella as well as vast bowls of garlic-infused spaghetti alle *vongole* (clams). The house

Pizzeria Tradizionale.

wines can be a bit rough but there are decent Chiantis and Sonves on the wine list. There's always plenty of backchat between waiting staff and guests and the noise really ratchets up as the night goes on. Altogether a fun night out.

Ripa di Porta Ticinese 7. www.pizzeriatradizionale.com ℂ **02-839-5133.** Main courses 8.50€–18€. Open daily noon–2:30pm and 7pm–1am except Wednesdays (only open for dinner). Metro: Porta Genova.

Shopping

Milan *is* shopping. And Milan is expensive.

Milan is known the world over as one of the temples of high fashion, with the hallowed streets **Montenapoleone** and **Spiga** in the **Quadrilatero d'Oro** the most popular place of worship. Here D&G, Prada,

Upscale shopping in Milan.

Gucci, Hermès, Louis Vuitton, Armani, Ralph Lauren, Versace, and Cavalli all jostle for customers among Milan's minted fashionistas. More reasonable shopping areas include **Via Torino** and **Corso Buenos Aires,** where mid-range international brands proliferate; if you're clever you can also pick up a designer bargain at outlet store **Il Salvagente** (Via Fratelli Bronzetti 16; ✆ **02-7611-0328**).

Fashion is one Milanese obsession, food is another, and the *centro storico* has many superb delis from which to purchase the purest of olive oils and fine cheeses. **Peck** (Via Spadari 9; ✆ **02-802-3161**) is still the number-one gourmet spot, although competition is keen from **Buongusto** (Via Caminadella 2; ✆ **02-8645-2479**) for the freshest of pasta in many guises, and the huge new **Eataly** megastore in Piazza XXV Aprile (www.eataly.it) for all comestibles Italian. The **top floor of La Rinascente department store** in Piazza del Duomo is another haven for foodies, with its Obika mozzarella bar and fine selection of packaged Italian goods (as an added bonus, you get a close-up view of the Duomo).

English-language books are sold at **Feltrinelli Librerie**, **Mondadori Multicenter,** and **Rizzoli** (all in and around Piazza del Duomo or inside the galleria) along with mobile and camera accessories. English-language newspapers can be found on most major newsstands around the *centro storico*.

MILANO MARKETS

Everybody loves a bargain, and there's no better place to find one than at the colorful, chaotic **Viale Papiniano market** (Metro: Sant'Agostino). Its sprawl of stalls are open Tuesday and Saturday; some flog designer seconds, others leather basics. **Flea markets** spring up on Saturdays along Alzaia Naviglio Grande (Metro: Porta Genova) and Fiera di Sinigaglia (Metro: Porta Genova), and on Sundays at San Donato Metro stop. The most historic is the Christmas extravaganza **Oh Bej! Oh Bej!** (roughly, Oh so nice! Oh so nice!), which seasonally takes over the *centro storico* around Sant'Ambrogio and Parco Sempione, selling everything from leather bags to handcrafted jewelry. A large **food market** at the Piazza Wagner metro stop is open every morning except Sunday. One Saturday a month, a Slow Food outdoor market is held in the courtyard of **Fabbrica Vapore** in north Milan (Via Procaccini 4; www.fabbricadelvapore.org).

Nightlife & Entertainment

Unless you're heading for the Ticinese and Navigli, Milan is a dressy city and generally looks askance at scruffy jeans and sneakers after dark. When most people don't dine until well after 10pm, it's not surprising that clubs and bars stay open until the very wee hours.

Milan has its share of glitzy clubs and cocktail bars, but most explode on the scene and disappear just

To keep up with Milan's ever-changing nightlife, check out **"Hello Milano"** (www.hellomilano.it/hm), which is published monthly and available in most hotels.

as quickly. A few spots that appear to be in for the long haul include the vine-covered cocktail terrace at **10 Corso Como** (www.10corsocomo.com; ☏ **02-2901-3581**), the evergreen dance club **Hollywood** (www.discotecahollywood.it; ☏ **02-6555-318**), and mega-club **Plastic** at Via Gargano 15 (no phone). A new kid on the block, **Ceresio 7 Pools & Restaurant** (www.ceresio7.com; ☏ **02-310-392-21**) offers a novel setup: a chic, sleek rooftop lounge with two pools

An orchestral performance at the famed Teatro Alla Scala.

where one can enjoy a cocktail while enjoying amazing views of the city.

North of Parco Sempione, **Chinatown** is a great area to explore for the dim sum restaurants concentrated around Via Paolo Sarpi. Just north of there, the **Fabbrica del Vapore** (Steam Factory; Via Procaccini 4, www.fabbricadelvapore.org; no phone) is an exciting arts venue featuring concerts and exhibition such as the visually stunning 2014 show "Van Gogh Live."

A venerable Milan institution, the **Conservatorio di Musica Giuseppe Verdi** has two stages for classical concerts, at Via Conservatorio 12 (www.consmilano.it; ✆ **02-762-110;** box office open Mon–Fri 8am–8pm). Yet Milan is forever associated with the grand old dame of opera, **Teatro Alla Scala,** perhaps the world's favorite opera house. La Scala is all decked out with sumptuous red seats, boxes adorned with gilt, and chandeliers dripping crystal. Tickets are hard to come by, so book well in advance of the opera season, kicking off on December 7 each year. Book online at www.teatroallascala.org, pay by phone with a credit card (✆ **02-861-778**), or go to La Scala's booking office in the Galleria del Sagrato, Piazza del Duomo, which is open from noon to 6pm daily (closed Aug). The ticket office at the opera house (Via Filodrammatici 2) releases 140 last-minute tickets for that evening's performance 2½ hours before the curtain goes up; get there promptly if you want a ticket.

BERGAMO

5

Bergamo is a city of two distinct characters. The ancient **Città Alta** is a beautiful medieval and Renaissance town perched on a green hill. **Città Bassa,** mostly built in the 19th and 20th century, sits at the feet of the upper town and concerns itself with getting on with 21st-century life. Visitors tend to focus on the historic upper town, which is largely a place for wandering, soaking in its rarified atmosphere, and enjoying the lovely vistas from its belvederes.

47km (29 miles) northeast of Milan.

Essentials

GETTING THERE **Trains** arrive from and depart for Milan Stazione Centrale hourly (50 min.; 5.50€).

Bus services to and from Milan are run by **Nord Est Trasporti** (www.nordesttrasporti.it; © **800-905-150**) and run at least hourly, with more services at commuter times; journey time is an hour and fares are 5.65€. The Z301 bus leaves from the Beltrami-Cairoli stop near Piazza Cadorna.

If you are driving, Bergamo is linked to Milan via the A4. The trip takes under an hour if traffic is good. Note: It's difficult to park in the largely pedestrianized Città Alta—park instead in Città Bassa and take the funicular (see p. 84) up to the historic area.

FACING PAGE: **Cathedral Santa Maria Maggiore.**

VISITOR INFORMATION The **Città Bassa tourist office** is close to the train and bus stations at Viale Papa Giovanni XXIII 57 (② **035-210-204**); it's open daily 9am to 12:30pm and 2 to 5:30pm. The **Città Alta office** is at Via Gombito, 13 (② **035-242-226**), right off Via Colleoni, and is open daily 9am–5:30pm. The **Bergamo Card** costs 10€ for 24 hours or 15€ for 2 days, but only makes sense if you plan to visit all the museums, as the churches are all free to enter. Check the website **www.comune.bergamo.it** for more information.

CITY LAYOUT Piazza Vecchia, the Colleoni Chapel, and most major sights are in the **Città Alta,** which is dissected by **Via Colleoni.** To reach **Piazza Vecchia** from the funicular station at **Piazza Mercato delle Scarpi,** it's a 5-minute stroll along **Via Gombito.** The Accademia Carrara is in the Città Bassa.

GETTING AROUND Bergamo has an efficient **bus system** that runs throughout the Città Bassa and to points around the Città Alta; tickets are 1.30€ for 90 minutes of travel and are available from the machines at the bus stops outside the train station or at the bus station opposite.

To reach the Città Alta from the train station, take bus no. 1 or 1A (clearly marked Città Alta on the front) and make the free transfer to the **Funicolare Bergamo Alta,** run by ATB Bergamo (Largo Porta Nuova; www.atb. bergamo.it; ② **035-236-026**), connecting the upper and lower cities. It runs every 7 minutes from 7am to 1:20am.

Exploring the Città Bassa

Most visitors scurry through Bergamo's lower, newer town on their way to the Città Alta, but you may want to pause long enough to explore its main thoroughfare, **Corso Sentierone,** with its mishmash of architectural styles (16th-century porticos, the Mussolini-era Palazzo di Giustizia, and two mock Doric temples); it's a

Lombardy & the Lake District

pleasant place to linger over espresso in a pavement cafe. The **Accademia Carrara** (Piazza Giacomo Carrara 82, www.lacarrara.it; ✆ **035-234396**) is worth a peek for its fine collection of Raphaels, Bellinis, Botticellis, and Canolettos. Città Bassa's 19th-century **Teatro Gaetano Donizetti** (Piazza Cavour 14) is the hub of Bergamo's lively cultural scene, with a fall opera season and a winter-to-spring season of dramatic performances; for details, call the theater at ✆ **035-416-0611** (www.teatrodonizetti.it).

Exploring the Città Alta

Crammed with *palazzi,* monuments, and churches, the Città Alta centers on two hauntingly beautiful adjoining squares, **the piazzas Vecchia** and **del Duomo.** Bergamasco strongman Bartolomeo Colleoni gave his name to the Città Alta's delightful main street, cobblestoned and so narrow you can almost touch the buildings on either side in places. It's lined with gorgeous shoe shops, posh delis, and classy confectioners.

The **Piazza Vecchia** looks like something out of one of local hero Gaetano Donizetti's opera sets; this hauntingly beautiful square was the hub of Bergamo's political and civic life from medieval times. The 12th-century **Palazzo della Ragione** (Court of Justice) was built by the Venetians, and its three graceful ground-floor arcades are embellished with the Lion of Saint Mark, symbol of the Venetian Republic, visible above the tiny 16th-century balcony and reached by a covered staircase to the right of the palace. Across the piazza, there's the **Biblioteca Civica (Public Library)**.

Walk through the archways of the Palazzo della Ragione to reach **Piazza del Duomo** and the **Basilica di Santa Maria Maggiore ★★**, (www.fondazionemia. it/basilica_s_maria_maggiore_bergamo/index.asp;

© 035-223-327). The basilica itself is entered through an ornate portico supported by Venetian lions; the interior is a masterpiece of ornately Baroque giltwork hung with Renaissance tapestries. Bergamo native son Gaetano Donizetti, the popular opera composer, is entombed here in a marble sarcophagus that's as excessive as the rest of the church's decor. An octagonal Baptistery in the piazza outside was originally inside the church but was removed and reconstructed in the 19th century. The oft-forgotten Tempietto of Santa Croce, tucked to the left of the basilica entrance, is worth seeking out for its endearing fragments of fresco of "The Last Supper." From April through October the basilica is open Tuesday to Saturday 9am to 12:30pm and 2:30 to 6pm, and Sunday 9am to 1pm and 3 to 6pm; November through March it's open Tuesday through Saturday 9am to 12:30pm and 2:30 to 5pm. Admission is free.

Most impressive, however, is the **Cappella Colleoni ★★★** (Piazza del Duomo; © **035-210-061;** free admission), found to the right of the basilica doors and entered through a highly elaborate pink-and-white marble facade. Bartolomeo Colleoni was a Bergamasco *condottiero* (mercenary) who fought for the Venetians; as a reward for his loyalty he was given Bergamo as his own private fiefdom in 1455. His elaborate funerary chapel was designed by Giovanni Antonio Amadeo,

Capella Colleoni

who created the Certosa di Pavia (see p. 59). Colleoni lies beneath a ceiling frescoed by Tiepolo and surrounded by statuary. Cappella Colleoni is open March to October daily from 9am to 12:30pm and 2 to 6:30pm; and November to February Tuesday to Sunday 9am to 12:30pm and 2 to 4:30pm.

Where to Stay & Eat

The charms of Bergamo's Città Alta are no secret and hotel rooms are in great demand over the summer, so make reservations well in advance. If you're staying in Milan, the city is an easy hour's journey from Stazione Centrale, making a perfect day trip.

Caffè della Funicolare ★ CAFE   In the upper terminal of the funicular, this simple spot serves coffee, wine, beer, basic snacks, and now even more elaborate meals. Bag a table on the terrace looking straight down over Bergamo Bassa, for some of the best views in the upper town.

Via Porta Dipinta 1. www.caffe dellafunicolare.it. ℂ **035-210- 091.** Main courses 10€–15€, sandwiches 5€ and up. Daily 8am–2am.

Caffè del Tasso ★ CAFE   On the Città Alta's atmospheric main piazza, this charming spot began life as a tailor's shop, but it's been a cafe since 1581. Today it has the gently jaded, rather cozy air of a 1950s teashop, but service is smart and they're

Hotel Piazza Vecchio.

generous with their *aperitivo* snacks. Next door the gelateria does brisk trade in summer, while an early evening drink on the terrace in summer is just a step away from heaven.

Piazza Vecchia 3. ℂ **035-237-966.** Main courses 10€–18€. Open daily 8am–midnight.

Hotel Piazza Vecchio ★★ Just steps from the Piazza Vecchio in the historic Città Alta, this ancient townhouse has stone walls and beamed ceilings. The rooms are all simply furnished, but each has a sleek new bathroom. The quieter rooms are at the back of the hotel looking over a labyrinth of alleyways and rooftops.

Via Colleoni 3. www.hotelpiazzavecchia.it. ℂ **035-253-179.** 13 units. 120€–200€ double. Rates Include breakfast. **Amenities:** Wi-Fi (free).

Osteria della Birra ★★ ORGANIC BREWPUB A great find in the Città Alta, this microbrewery

Osteria della Birra.

restaurant offers a simple menu of *piadine* (flatbread) and *panini* stuffed full of local cured hams and artisanal cheeses. The *raison d'etre*, however, is the beer (no wine here). Part of the Elav microbrewery, this spot is run by a bunch of enthusiastic youngsters keen to promote their organic brew along with their largely organic produce.

Piazza Masheroni 1/c. www.elavbrewery.com/en/pubs/osteria-della-birra. ✆ **035-242-440.** Main courses 8€–15€. Mon–Fri noon–3pm, 6pm–2am; Sat–Sun noon–2am.

6

MANTUA
(MANTOVA)

One of Lombardy's best-kept secrets, Mantua is in the eastern reaches of the region, making it an easy side trip from Milan. Like its neighboring cities in Emilia-Romagna, Mantua owes its beautiful Renaissance monuments to one family, in this case the Gonzagas, who conquered the city in 1328 and ruled benevolently until 1707. They were avid collectors of art and ruled through the greatest centuries of Italian art; encounter the treasures they collected in the massive **Palazzo Ducale;** in their summer retreat, the **Palazzo Te;** and in the churches and piazzas that grew up around their court.

The Palazzo Ducale, the **Galleria Museo Palazzo Valenti Gonzaga**, and other monuments were recently restored, while Mantegna's famous **Camera degli Sposi** reopened in 2015 following earthquake damage in 2012 (see p. 96).

158km (98 miles) E of Milan, 62km (38 miles) N of Parma, 150km (93 miles) SW of Venice

Essentials

GETTING THERE Six direct **trains** depart daily from Milan Stazione Centrale (1 hr. 50 mins.; 11.50€). There are nine daily trains from Verona (30–40 min.; 3.75€).

PREVIOUS PAGE: **A nightscape of Mantua.**

The speediest highway connections from Milan are via the A4 autostrade to Verona, then the A22 from Verona to Mantua (about 2 hrs.).

VISITOR INFORMATION The **tourist office** at Piazza Mantegna 6 (www.turismo.mantova.it; ✆ **0376-432-432**) is open on weekends from 9am–5pm; during the week, the office is open 9am–1:30pm and 2:30–5pm (until 6pm in spring and summer). It's just to the right of the entrance to the basilica of Sant'Andrea.

CITY LAYOUT Mantua is tucked onto a fat finger of land surrounded on three sides by the **Mincio River,** which widens into a series of lakes, named prosaically **Lago Superiore, Lago di Mezzo,** and **Lago Inferiore.** Most of the sights are within an easy walk of one another within the compact center, which is a 15-minute walk northwards from the lakeside train station.

Exploring Mantua

Mantua is a place for wandering along arcaded streets and through cobbled squares with handsomely proportioned churches and *palazzi*.

The southernmost of these squares is **Piazza delle Erbe (Square of the Herbs) ★,** so named for its produce-and-food market. Mantua's civic might is clustered here in a series of late-medieval and early Renaissance structures that include the **Palazzo della Ragione (Courts of Justice)** and **Palazzo del Podestà (Mayor's Palace)** from the 12th and 13th centuries, and the **Torre dell'Orologio,** topped with a 14th-century astrological clock. Also on this square is Mantua's earliest religious structure, the **Rotunda di San Lorenzo,** a miniature round church from the 11th century (all of its building were closed for restoration and covered with scaffolding at the time of writing). The city's

Renaissance masterpiece, **Basilica di Sant'Andrea** (see below), is off to one side on Piazza Mantegna.

To the north, Piazza delle Erbe transforms into **Piazza Broletto** through a series of arcades; here a statue commemorates the poet Virgil, who was born in Mantova in 70 B.C. The next square, **Piazza Sordello,** is vast, cobbled, rectangular, and lined with well-restored medieval *palazzi* and the 13th-century Duomo. Most notable is the massive hulk of the **Palazzo Ducale** that forms the eastern wall of the piazza. To enjoy Mantua's lakeside views and walks, follow Via San Giorgio from the **Piazza Sordello** and turn right on to Lungolago dei Gonzaga, which leads back into the town center.

Tip: The **Mantua Museum Card** costs 15€ and allows access to five city museums for 15€, allowing a saving of several euros on normal admission charges. Visit **www.mantovaducale.beniculturali.it** for more details.

Basilica di Sant'Andrea ★★ CHURCH   A graceful Renaissance facade fronts this 15th-century

The splendid interior of the Basilica di Sant' Andrea.

church by star architect Leon Battista Alberti. The grandest church in Mantua, it is topped by a dome added by Filippo Juvarra in the 18th century. Inside, the vast classically proportioned space is centered on the church's single aisle. Light pours in through the dome, highlighting the carefully crafted *trompe l'oeil* painting of the coffered, barrel-vaulted ceiling. The Gonzagas' court painter Andrea Mantegna—creator of the Camera degli Sposi in the **Palazzo Ducale** (see below)—is buried in the first chapel on the left. The crypt houses a reliquary containing the blood of Christ, which was allegedly brought here by Longinus, the Roman soldier who thrust his spear into Jesus's side; this is processed through town on March 18, the feast of Mantua's patron, Sant'Anselmo.

Piazza Mantegna. www.santandreainmantova.it. Free admission. Daily 8am–noon, 3 7pm.

Museo di Palazzo Ducale ★★ PALACE The massive power base of the Gonzaga dynasty spreads over the northeast corner of Mantua, incorporating Piazza Sordello, the Romanesque-Gothic Duomo, the Castello San Giorgio, and the Palazzo Ducale. Together they form a private city connected by a labyrinth of corridors, ramps, courtyards, and staircases filled with Renaissance frescoes and ancient Roman sculptures. Behind the walls of this massive fortress-cum-family palace lies the history of Mantua's most powerful family and what remains of the treasure trove they amassed over the centuries. Between their skills as warriors and their penchant for marrying into wealthier houses, the Gonzagas acquired power, money, and the services of some of the top artists of the time, including Pisanello, Titian, and Andrea Mantegna.

The most fortunate of many opportunistic unions was in 1490, between Francesco II Gonzaga and aristocratic Isabella d'Este from Ferrara. It was she who commissioned many of the complex's art-filled apartments, including the incomparable **Camera degli Sposi** in the north tower of the Castello San Giorgio. This is the undoubted masterpiece of Andrea Mantegna, taking 9 years to complete. It provides a fascinating glimpse into late 15th-century courtly life.

The Palazzo Ducale offers up a glorious maze of gilded, frescoed, marble-floored rooms, passageways, corridors, secret gardens, follies, and scattered pieces of elaborate *intaglio* furniture. Standouts among all the excess include the Arturian legends ornamenting walls of **the Sala del Pisanello**, painted by Pisanello between 1436 and 1444; the **Sale degli Arazzi** (Tapestry Rooms) hung with copies of Raphael's tapestries in the Vatican; the **Galleria degli Specchi** (Hall of Mirrors); the low-ceilinged **Appartamento dei Nani** (Apartments of the Dwarfs), where a replica of the Holy Staircase in the Vatican is built to miniature scale; and the **Galleria dei Mesi** (Hall of the Months).

Piazza Sordello, 40. www.mantovaducale.beniculturali.it. ⓒ **0376-224-832** for ticket info. Admission 6.50 € for the Palazzo Ducale Museum; 12€ for the Castello San Giorgio + Corte Vecchia + Freddi Collection; 6.50€ for the Corte Vecchia + apartment of Isabella d'Este. Free admission to all on the first Sunday every month. Tues–Sun 8:15am–7:15pm. Last entrance at 6:20pm.

Palazzo Te ★★ PALACE   This glorious summer palace, designed by Giulio Romano between 1525 and 1535, took a decade to complete. Built for Federico II Gonzaga, the sybaritic son of Isabella d'Este (see above), this splendid Renaissance palace was his retreat from court life, and it was designed to indulge his obsessions. A tour leads through a series of evermore-lavishly adorned apartments, decorated by the best artists of the day. Gonzaga's enthusiasms for love and sex, astrology, and horses are evident throughout, from the almost 3-D effect in the **Hall of the Horses** to the sexually overt frescoes by Romano in the elaborate **Chamber of Amor and Psyche.** The greatest room in the palace, however, is a metaphor for Gonzaga power: In the **Sala dei Giganti (Room of the Giants),** Titan is overthrown by the gods in a dizzying display of architectural *trompe l'oeil* that gives the illusion that the ceiling is falling inwards. The Palazzo Te is also home of the **Museo Civico**, whose permanent collections on the upper floors include the Gonzaga family's coins, medallions, 20th-century family portraits by Armando Spadini, and a few Egyptian artifacts.

Viale Te 13. www.palazzote.it. © **0376-323-266.** Admission 10€ adults, 7€ seniors, 3.50€ ages 12–18 and students, free for under 12. Mon 1–6pm; Tues–Sun 9am–6pm. Audioquide 5€. Palazzo Te is a 20-minute walk from the center of Mantua along Via Principe Amedeo.

MORE MANTUA MUSEUMS

En route from the center of town to Palazza Te, you'll pass **Casa del Mantegna ★,** the house and studio of Andrea Mantegna, which is now an art gallery (Via Acerbi 47, © **0376-360-506;** Tues–Sun 10am–12:30pm, Tues–Wed 3–5pm, Sat–Sun 3–6pm; admission free). Close by in the stark white Palazzo Sebastiano, the **Museo della Città ★** (Largo XXIV Maggio 12; www.museodellacitta.mn.it; © **0376-367-087**; Mon 1–6pm, Tues–Sun 9am–6pm; admission 12€) gallops through the history of Mantua. Among its many architectural fragments and columns

Frescoed ceilings in Mantua's Palazzo Te.

is an impressive bust of Francesco Gonzaga, who commissioned the palace in 1507.

Just to the left of the Palazzo Ducale's main entrance, in the old markethall at the corner of Piazza Sordello, the **Museo Archeologico Nazionale di Mantova** houses in one giant space all sorts of local discoveries of Bronze Age, Greek, Etruscan, and Roman pottery, glassware, and utensils (www.museo archeologicomantova.beniculturali.it; *©* **0376-320-003;** admission 4€, age 17 and under free; Nov–Mar Tues–Sun 8:30am–1:30pm; Apr–Oct Tues, Thurs, Sat 1:30–7pm, Wed, Fri, Sun 8:30am–1:30pm.).

The lovely Baroque interior of the **Teatro Bibiena ★★** is also worth a peek for its rows of luxurious boxes. Find it at Via Accademia 47 (*©* **0376-327-653;** admission 2€, 17 and under free; Tues–Sun

10am–1pm and 3–6pm, except Sat–Sun 10am–6pm mid-Mar to mid-Nov.)

For a change of pace—if you can catch it open, which is usually on weekends—the **Galleria Storica dei Vigili del** Fuoco (Fire Engine Museum) ★ at Largo Vigili del Fuoco 1 (www.vigilfuoco.it; ✆ **0376-227-71**) has plenty of historic engines to distract from ancient art. Call beforehand to check opening times.

Where to Eat & Stay

Like Milan, Mantua sees many expense-account business travelers during the week, with families and tourists flocking in for the weekends and over summer, so book rooms in the town center well ahead of time.

Caffè Caravatti ★ CAFE   Join the Mantovese for a lunchtime pick-me-up after a morning of shopping in the gorgeous arcaded streets of the old city. The old-fashioned brass and wood bar is lined with mysterious local liqueurs while glasses of prosecco and Campari cocktails are dispensed at the speed of light.
Via Broletto 16. ✆ **0376-327-826.** Mon–Thurs 7am–8:30pm, Fri–Sat 7am–midnight.

Caffè Modi ★ ITALIAN   Named for louche artist Amedeo Modigliani, whose moody portrait dominates the restaurant, Modi is a casual and friendly stop on the tourist circuit around Piazza Sordello. Chill music plays and threadbare armchairs lend a bohemian charm to the place. The menu is predictable in its selection of local pasta dishes and vast mountains of salad, but they are all well presented and tasty. If the place is quiet, the lovely laidback owner will come and chat—mostly about her enthusiasm for the works of

Modigliani. Concerts and recitals are held here from time to time.

Via San Giorgio 4. ☎ **0376-181-0111.** Main courses 8€–15€. Wed–Mon noon–3pm, 7:15pm–midnight.

Il Scalco Grasso ★★ MODERN ITALIAN This contemporary bistro with a minimalist black-and-red decor is owned by a young chef keen to push boundaries. Expect beautifully created vegetarian dishes—local pasta stuffed with marrow squash, delicate risotto, or perhaps a superb chickpea soup flavored with squid—alongside menu items like tartare of veal, pike, beef cheek, and local delicacy stracotto d'asino (donkey stew). Some lovely Lugano wines are available by the glass or bottle, and little bites of delicacies are happily produced for guests to sample before ordering. A sophisticated choice, with reservations recommended for weekends.

Via Trieste 55. www.scalcograssomantova.it. ☎ **349-374-7958.** Main courses 18€–30€. Daily noon–2:30pm and 7:30–10pm (until 11:30pm Fri–Sat); except no lunch Mon, no dinner Sun.

Osteria dell'Oca ★★★ LOMBARDY The restaurant "of the duck" is crammed nightly with locals enjoying vibrant local cooking at truly amazing prices. This is an Italian family-run restaurant at its very best: noisy, happy, and joyous. The best *primi* are the sharing plates of *peccati di gola*, local salamis and pancetta accompanied by a thick wedge of creamy polenta, lard, and beetroot salsa. Other specialties are ravioli stuffed with marrow and pike pulled fresh from the lakes surrounding the city. Only three wines are served, in chunky carafes. Opt for the white from local vineyards rather than the *lambrusco,* which is overly sweet. This generous outpouring of food is rounded off with complimentary coffees and the thick, treacle-like hazelnut *digestivo della casa*. Book ahead for a weekend table.

Via Trieste 10. www.osteriadellocamantova.com. ☎ **0376-327-171.** Main courses 12€–17€. Wed–Sat and Mon noon–3pm and 7:15–11:30pm, Sun noon–3pm.

Casa Poli ★★★

Hidden behind the facade of a 19th-century mansion, this bijou boutique hotel is packed night after night with both business travelers and holidaymakers. It's easy to see why. Guest rooms are spotless and stylishly pared down in contemporary style, with funky lights, bright splashes of color, and equally cool bathrooms. The lounge is full of arty books, and the pretty summer courtyard is a great spot to while away an hour over an evening *aperitivo*. But it's the staff that really makes this place shine; they're chatty and informal, and all willing to go that extra mile to accommodate guest requests.

Corso Garibaldi 32. www.hotelcasapoli.it. ☎ **0376-288-170.** 27 units. 118€–170€ double. Rates include continental breakfast. Free street parking. **Amenities:** Bar; concierge; Wi-Fi (free).

Residenza Bibiena ★★

Tucked away in a pretty corner of Mantua's *centro storico* 5 minutes from the Palazzo Ducale, this cozy B&B, located in a traditional terracotta townhouse, has a pleasing air of old-school charm. The rooms are very simply furnished with wooden furniture and tiled floors enlivened by warm color schemes and pretty bed linens. Vast family rooms are available, the en suites are all huge by Italian standards, and a couple of rooms have terraces. Breakfast is served in the bar across the road.

Piazza Arche, 5. www.residenzabibiena.it. ☎ **0376-355-699.** 5 units. 80€ double. Rates include breakfast. Parking 15€. **Amenities:** Wi-Fi (free).

Shopping & Entertainment

The favored shopping streets in Mantua radiate off Piazza delle Erbe, a delightful cluster of cobbled and arcaded streets sheltering delis stuffed with local cheeses, hams, fresh pasta, and olive oils. **Corso Umberto, Via Verdi,** and **Via Oberdan** are lined with classy boutiques, smart shoe shops, and bookstores. There's a **farmers' market** on Lungorio IV di Novembre on Saturday, and come

A street vendor at the Golosaria Food Fair.

lunchtime the lines outside the delicatessens form as happy patrons leave with beautifully packaged goodies. It's perfect fodder for a picnic in the lakeside gardens along Lungolago dei Gonzaga.

Mantua is a cultured city well supplied with theater and classical concerts; there are regular recitals at cute little **Teatro Bibiena** and a full program of films and concerts at **Mantova Teatro** in the Piazza Cavallotti (www.teatrosocialemantova.it). A chamber-music festival is held every May and the **Festivaletteratura literature festival** each September.

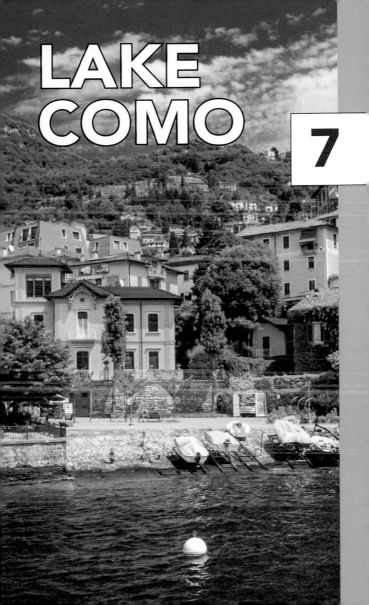

LAKE COMO

ife is slower around the northern Italian lakes than in mega-paced Milan. The city of Como is an ideal base for drawing breath and kicking back. Sitting on the southwestern tip of Lake Como, the city is essentially a center of commerce with a miniscule medieval quarter and a pretty waterfront. Tourists flock here for its ancient heritage, fine churches, and lake views. From there, frequent ferry service hops around the lake, visiting its many romantic lakeshore villas and villages.

Essentials

GETTING THERE **Trains** run from Milan's Stazione Central and Porta Garibaldi half-hourly to Como San Giovanni; the trip takes 1 hour and costs

Como (town): 65km (40 miles) NE of Milan; Menaggio: 35km (22 miles) NE of Como and 85km (53 miles) N of Milan; Varenna: 50km (31 miles) NE of Como and 80km (50 miles) NE of Milan

4.80€. One-hour services from Milan Cadorna arrive at Como Nord Lago (just off the lakefront promenade, near the ferry point) and cost 4.80€.

VISITOR INFORMATION The **regional tourist office** at Piazza Cavour 17 (www.lakecomo.com; ✆ **031-269-712**) dispenses a wealth of information on hotels, restaurants, and campgrounds around the lake. The office is open Monday to Saturday 9am to 1pm and 2 to 5pm. You'll also find tourist offices open in summer in several

PREVIOUS PAGE: **The town of Varenna on Lake Como.**

Como's Duomo.

of the small towns around the lake; in **Tremezzo** at Via Regina 3 (☏ **0344-40-493**); in **Varenna** at Via IV Novembre 7 (www.varennaitaly.com; ☏ **0341-830-367**); and in **Bellaggio** at Piazza Mazzini (www.bellagio lakecomo.com; ☏ **0341-950-204**).

GETTING AROUND Como is the jumping-off point for most adventures on Lake Como, which is criss-crossed by regular **ferry routes:** It takes 4 hours to travel from one end to the other and there are many stops along the way. The most popular are **Tremezzo, Menaggio, Bellagio,** and timeless **Varenna** (see p. 109). Single fares from Como are 10.40€ to Bellagio; a day pass costs 28€. Tickets cannot be purchased online. The ferry terminal, run by **Navigazione Lago di Como,** is on the lake esplanade at Via per Cernobbio 18 (www.navigazionelaghi.it; ☏ **031-579-211**).

Como ★★

Como's tiny *centro storico* is dominated by the flam boyant **Duomo ★★** (Piazza Duomo; www.cattedral edicomo.it; ☏ **031-331-2275**), which combines Gothic and Renaissance architecture for two very different facades; long, narrow windows and a Gothic stained-glass rose window mark the western end, with a seamless apse and Baroque dome added in 1744 by architect Filippo Juvarra at the eastern end. The Duomo is open daily 10:30am to 5pm (visitors are welcome from 1pm to 4:30pm on Sundays after mass) and admission is free.

Two blocks south of the Duomo, the 12th-century **San Fedele** ★ basilica (free admission; daily 8am–noon, 3:30–7pm), stands above a charming square of the same name. Parts of the five-sided church, including the altar, date from the 6th century, and there are some fine frescoes along the right-hand side aisle.

Como's main street, **Corso Vittorio Emanuele II,** cuts through the medieval quarter and has plenty of upmarket boutiques and classy delis. If you have time, take the 10-minute **funicular ride** from Lungo Lario Trieste up to hilltop **Brunate ★★,** which has a cluster of excellent restaurants and bars. The funicular runs up a steep cliff-side, with glorious views of Lake Como glinting below; at the top, you'll also find wooded hiking trails that lead up to Bellagio. The funicular ticket office is at Piazza de Gasperi 4 (www.funicolarecomo.it; ℂ **031-303-608;** daily 8am–10:30pm; funicular runs until midnight on Saturdays and in summer). Tickets are 3€ adults, 2€ for kids under 12 (children under 110cm in height travel free). Trains depart both ends of line every 30 minutes.

Lake Como's Waterfront Villages

The romantic waterfront villages of Lake Como, with their cute clusters of yellow and pink houses, majestic *palazzos,* and lush lakeside gardens, are easily explored by ferry (see p. 105) or by car. Here are a few of the highlights, going clockwise round the lake.

The harbor of Lenno.

LENNO ★★★ For centuries Lake Como was the playground of privileged Lombardian aristocrats (and quite honestly not much has changed); **Villa del Balbianello** at Lenno (Via Comoedia 5; http://eng.fondo ambiente.it/beni/villa-del-balbianello-fai-properties. asp; ✆ **0344-56-110**), is one of the best known of their fabulous villas, with ornate landscaped gardens and a 16th-century palace sitting high on its peninsula over the lake. (You may recognize it from its recent brush with fame in the Bond movie *Casino Royale*.) The interior is full of priceless French furniture complemented by eclectic artwork from the travels of its former owner, explorer Guido Monzino, who died in 1988 and left the villa to the Italian National Trust. Admission varies: Garden entrance only is 7€ adults, 3€ kids 4 to 12; garden and villa (with compulsory tour) is 13€ adults, 7€ children aged 4–12. (***Tip:*** There's a discount if you reserve in advance.) Open mid-March to mid-November, 10am to 6pm, closed Monday and Wednesday.

The gardens of Villa Carlotta.

TREMEZZO ★★ On the western side of Lake Como, Tremezzo was the prestigious 19th-century retreat of the Italian aristocracy; today it is lorded over by the exceptionally expensive **Grand Hotel Tremezzo** (www.grandhoteltremezzo.com; ℓ **0344-42-491**) and its wonderfully stylish lido on the lake. The luxuriant gardens, museum, and rich art collections of the ornate 17th-century **Villa Carlotta** are open to the public (Via Regina 2; www.villacarlotta.it; ℓ **0344-404-05**). Admission is 9€ adults, 7€ seniors, 5€ students. Open late March to mid-October from 9am to 7:30pm (last entry 6pm); open late October to mid-March from 10am to 6pm (last entry 5pm).

BELLANO ★ Most people stop in Bellano on the eastern shores of Lake Como to visit the **Orrido** (ℓ **338-5246-716;** admission 3€ adults, 2.50€ seniors and under 14), a deep gorge cut out of the cliffs by the River Pioverna as it tears down the hillside. A nighttime trip down the floodlit gorge is a rare and eerie treat, and one that appears to be under threat from recent hydroelectric plans that will reduce the flow of the torrent. Opening times vary seasonally but are roughly: April to June and September 10am to 1pm and 2:30 to 7pm; July to August 10am to 7pm and 8:45 to 10pm.

VARENNA ★★★ Adorable Varenna gives Bellagio a run for its money as the prettiest village on Lake Como, with a tumble of pink and terracotta houses in a labyrinth of narrow, cobbled streets, and smart villas clustered around the shoreline. Its winding lakeside path hangs over the water, with bars, shops, and art galleries looking over the lake. Linger a while over a glass of prosecco and watch the sun go down over the glittering water.

BELLAGIO ★★★ Photogenic Bellagio is the most popular destination around Lake Como and has just about remained on the right side of overtly touristic. The shady lakefront promenade is lined with chic hotels, bars, and cafes. Pretty medieval alleyways ascend from the lake in steep steps and are lined with souvenir stores selling expensive hand-tooled leather accessories. Just don't expect too many bargains. Regardless of the multitude of tourists, this is

The narrow streets of Bellagio.

still a lovely place to linger for lunch overlooking the lake.

Where to Eat & Stay

With Como's fame has come a paucity of decent moderately priced hotels, although there are still plenty of options around the lake. If you're looking for a splurge, Cernobbio is home to one of Italy's most exclusive and expensive hotels: the **Villa d'Este** (see p. 112). The local cuisine draws heavily on the lake, and polenta is as popular here as pasta.

Da Pietro ★★ PASTA AND PIZZA   There are several touristy restaurants on Como's gorgeous Piazza del Duomo, all in a row and fairly interchangeable, but Da Pietro has long had the edge for friendliness and smooth service. It's a perfect family pitstop for a lunch of decently cooked pasta or vast, crisp pizzas. You pay for the peerless view of the Duomo, but the atmosphere is buzzing night and day.

Piazza Duomo 16, Como. ✆ **031-264-005.** Main courses around 12€. Daily 10am–midnight.

La Polenteria ★★★ REGIONAL ITALIAN   Vegetarians, be prepared to take pot luck, as the ethos behind La Polenteria is to utilize and cook whatever is in season; this could be anything from snails, venison, wild boar, and fish fresh from the lake to porcini mushrooms, or, in fall, pasta flavored with chestnuts. As the name suggests, the regional specialty polenta (cornmeal) accompanies many of the dishes. The rustic dining room has had a facelift; gone are the shelves of dusty bottles and farming implements hanging on the walls. Now they are a cheery, warming yellow. Booking is advisable and proceedings can get riotous in the evening.

Via Scalini, 66, Brunate. www.lapolenteria.it. ✆ **031-336-5105.**
Main courses 8€–30€. Fri 7:15–10:30pm, Sat–Sun 12:15pm–
2:30pm, 7:30–10:30pm.

Splendide Ristorante ★★★ REGIONAL ITAL-
IAN   There's not a prettier spot on the whole of Lake
Como than this geranium-filled terrace belonging to
the Hotel Excelsior Splendide in Bellagio. Hanging
out over the shimmering waters of the lake, the restaurant concentrates on good local dishes, from polentas
and pasta to giant prawns sizzled in garlic and fresh
trout from the lake. There's also a delicious ice cream
bar under the arcade across the street.

Via Lungo Lario Manzoni 28, Bellagio. www.hsplendide.com.
✆ **031-950-225.** Main courses 10€–40€. Mar–Nov noon–
2:30pm.

Hotel du Lac ★★   With one entrance slap bang on
Varenna's charming waterfront and the other hidden
away in its equally photogenic tangle of alleyways, the
Hotel du Lac is housed in an elegant 19th-century
villa offering prized views across Lake Como. It's now
open for "light lunch," and the flower-filled terrace is
the perfect spot for cocktails à deux as the sun sinks
over the lake. The romantic theme continues inside
with marble pillars and wrought-iron staircases, roomy
(for Europe) bedrooms decked out in subtle shades of
green, gold, and red, plus revamped bathrooms.

Via del Prestino 11, Varenna. www.albergodulac.com. ✆ **0341-
830-238.** 16 units. Doubles 175€–260€. Rates include breakfast. Closed mid-Nov to Feb. Free parking. **Amenities:**
Restaurant (lunch only); bar; Wi-Fi (free).

Hotel Paradiso sul Largo ★★★   This great
albergo has had a total overhaul since it reopened in

2008 and is now powered by voltaic panels, making it the first eco-hotel around Lake Como. Right at the top of the village of Brunate above Como town, it's in a little *piazza* surrounded by restaurants and is on the edge of pleasingly untamed forested countryside. The rooms are simple, spotlessly clean, and functional, but the main selling points are the amazing hilltop views over Lake Como from the breakfast room, and the panoramic terrace with swimming pool and Jacuzzi. Be sure to book a room with lake views.

Via Scalini 74, Brunate San Maurizio. www.hotelparadisosullago.com. ✆ **031-364-099.** 12 units. 137€ double. Rates include breakfast. Free parking. **Amenities:** Pizza restaurant; bar; outdoor pool; shuttle service; Wi-Fi (free).

Nest on the Lake ★★   This cute little B&B is in a tranquil lakeside spot in Lezzeno, minutes from Bellagio (see p. 109). Bedrooms are all decked out in white, some with four-poster beds, and all have wrought-iron balconies. A decent self-service breakfast is offered, and the more-than-helpful Raffa and Tino are building quite a reputation for their hospitality; they are happy to recommend restaurants and organize tours. The minimum stay is 3 nights in summer.

Frazione Sostra 17/19, Lezzeno. www.nestonthelake.com. ✆ **031-914-372.** 5 units. 100–110€ double; 120–140€ apt. Parking 5€ per day. **Amenities:** Solarium; Wi-Fi (free).

Villa d'Este ★★   Set in an ornate Renaissance *palazzo* dating from 1568 and overlooking Lake Como amid verdant parklands, the Villa d'Este certainly adds

The Villa d'Este.

to the lake's reputation as playboy central. It sees a constant procession of celebs and minor royalty arriving by speedboat or helicopter to luxuriate in the raft of sporting facilities, the array of fine dining options, and the refined rooms furnished with priceless antiques. As befits one of the most exclusive hotels in the world, two revamped private villas guarantee complete seclusion from the hoi polloi.

Via Regina 40, Cernobbio. www.villadeste.com. ✆ **031-3481.** 152 units. 440€–760€ double; 880€–970€ junior suite. Rates include breakfast. Free parking. Closed mid-Nov to mid-Mar. **Amenities:** 3 restaurants; 3 bars; nightclub; indoor and outdoor pools; spa; concierge; Wi-Fi (free).

8

LAKE MAGGIORE

Maggiore lies west of Como, a long, thin wisp of a lake protected by mountains and fed by the River Ticino, which flows on to Milan. Roughly a quarter of the northern section of the lake stands in Switzerland, including the city of Locarno and its delightful satellite resort of **Ascona. Stresa** is the largest town on the Italian part of the lake, a timeless resort on the western shoreline, famed for its position opposite the **Isole Borromee** islands. Regular **ferries** span Maggiore and there are frequent stops on the way from **Arona,** south of Stresa; the most popular include **Luino** for its massive market, and **Laveno** for cable-car rides up to mountain panoramas (see p. 120).

(see p. 120)

Stresa: 90km (56 miles) NW of Milan

Essentials

GETTING THERE Stresa is linked with Milan Stazione Centrale and Porta Garibaldi by 20 **trains** a day. Journeys take around an hour and cost 8.30€.

Boats arrive at and depart from Piazza Marconi, Stresa. Many lakeside spots can be reached from Stresa, with most boats on the lake operated by **Navigazione Laghi** (www.navlaghi.it; © **0322-233-200**). The lake's main ferry office, however, is at the lake's southern tip in

FACING PAGE: **Grand Hotel des Iles Borromee on Lake Maggiore.**

Arona, at Viale Baracca 1; from there, ferries to Stresa take 40 minutes and cost 6.20€.

The A8 runs west from Milan to Sesto Calende, near the southern end of the lake; from there, follow Route SS33 up the western shore to Stresa. The trip takes just over an hour, but much longer on a summer weekend.

VISITOR INFORMATION Stresa's **tourist office** is at the ferry dock on Piazza Marconi (www.stresaturismo. it; ✆ **0323-30-150**) and is open daily 10am to 12:30pm and 3 to 6:30pm (mid-October to mid-March closed Sat afternoons and Sun). For hiking information, ask for the booklet "Percorsi Verdi."

Stresa & the Islands

The biggest town on the Italian side of Maggiore, elegant Stresa is the springboard to the Isole Borromee (Borromean Islands), the tiny Baroque jewels of the lake. Now a genteel tourist town, Stresa captured the hearts of 19th-century aristocracy, who settled in droves in grandiose villas strung along the promenade.

Fishing village Isola dei Pescatori.

Just back into the tangle of medieval streets, **Piazza Cadorna** is a mass of restaurants that spill out into the center of the square in summer. There's a food and craft market on summer Thursday afternoons along the promenade, and a lido and beach club on the lakefront.

The three Isole Borromee are named for the aristocratic Borromeo family who has owned them since the 12th century. Public **ferries** leave for the islands every half-hour from Stresa's Piazza Marconi outside the tourist office, a 16.90€ **daily pass** is the most economical way to visit the Bella, Pescatori, and Madre islands all in one day. For more information on the Borromean Islands, check out www.isoleborromee.it.

ISOLA DEI PESCATORI ★★ Pescatori is stuck in a medieval time warp, with ancient fishermens' houses clustered together on every inch of the tiny island. Wander the meandering cobbled streets as they reveal tiny churches, art galleries, souvenir shops, pizza and pasta restaurants, and, at every turn, a glimpse of the lake beyond. It's an entrancing place to explore, but be warned: the prices are extortionate and the crowds frustrating.

ISOLA BELLA ★★★ The minute islet of Bella is dominated by the massive Baroque **Palazzo Borromeo** (www.isoleborromee.it) with its formal Italianate gardens. It makes for an absorbing tour, with conspicuous displays of wealth evident in the rich decor and exquisite furnishings. The terraced gardens, restored in 2014, are dotted with follies and have spectacular views across Maggiore. Of special interest are the ornate grottoes underground where the Borromeos went to stay cool, or the painting gallery, hung with 130 of the most important artworks the Borromeos collected over the centuries. Admission is 15€ adults, 8.50€ for ages 6 to 15. Open mid-Mar to mid-Oct 9am–5:30pm.

Isola Bella.

ISOLA MADRE ★★ The largest and most peaceful of the islands is Isola Madre (30 min. from Stresa), overspread with exquisite flora in the 3.2-hectare (8-acre) **Orto Botanico.** Pick up a map at the ticket office to identify all the rhododendrons, camellias, and ancient wisteria. Many a peacock and fancy pheasant stalk across the lawns of another 16th-century **Borromeo palazzo** (www.isoleborromee.it), which is filled with family memorabilia and some interesting old puppet-show stages. Admission to the garden and palace is 12€ adults, 6.50€ for ages 6 to 15. Open Mar–Oct 9am–5:30pm.

Around Lake Maggiore

Beyond Stresa, Maggiore offers natural beauty and architectural wonders as well as lively towns, markets, and cable-car rides up into the mountains.

Arona ★★ As well as having the lake's main ferry office (see p. 116) this sophisticated town at the southern end of Lake Maggiore is a shopping magnet, with its charming **Via Cavour** lined with elegant boutiques and expensive delicatessens. The giant bronze **statue of Carlo Borromeo** (see p. 120), who was born in Arona in 1538, is located just outside of town. It's so huge, you can even climb inside and gaze out at the lake through Carlo's eyes (✆ **0322-249-669;** admission 5€; mid-Mar to Oct daily 9am–noon and 2–6pm).

Luino ★★ On the western shore of Lake Maggiore just a few miles from the Swiss border, Luino is home of one of northern Italy's most popular **street markets**, with more than 350 stalls taking over the town every Wednesday. Here you'll find cheery sarongs, spices, piles of salami, grappas, olive oils, as well as the hand-tooled leather belts and bags for which the region is famous. Day visitors from Milan can catch the train directly to Luino from Milan's Stazione Centrale or Stazione Porta Garibaldi in under 2 hours (7.90€), while extra ferries serve the town every

View of Lake Maggiore from the peak of Sasso del Fero.

Italy's Medieval Oligarchs

The all-powerful Borromeo family were Lombardian aristocrats who played a major part in Milanese politics and religion for 200 years. They regarded the vast tracts of land around the southern end of Lake Maggiore as their own personal fiefdom, where they built castles, monuments, and palaces. The family spawned several archbishops of Milan, including Federico (1564–1631) and Carlo (1538–1584), a singularly wily and wealthy individual who was canonized in 1610 for his support of the Counter-Reformation against papal infallibility. A great bronze statue of Carlo stands in Arona, on a hillock looking out across the lake to his former family home, Rocca Borromeo at Angera.

Wednesday. Check ferry timetables with www.navlaghi.it.

Sasso del Fero ★★★   East of the lakeshore town of Laveno, make for Laveno Mombello, where you can take the 16-minute **cable-car** trip (www.funiviedellagomaggiore.it; ✆ **0332-668-012;** 10€ roundtrip) up the lush Val Cuvia to the Poggia Sant'Elsa viewpoint atop **Sasso del Ferro**, towering 1,062m (3,484 ft.) over Lake Maggiore. Here you'll find truly breathtaking panoramas, looking west to the snow-capped Alps or south over the mini-lakes Varese, Monate, and Comabbio. If the conditions are right, there'll be plenty of paragliders to watch, and the hills are crisscrossed with scenic hiking trails. Leave time to relax over a prosecco in the **Ristorante Albergo Funivia** (see p. 123). Opening times vary according to weather conditions, but the cable car generally runs April to October (Mon–Fri 11am–6:30pm; Sat–Sun 11am–10:30pm).

Santa Caterina del Sasso Ballaro.

Santa Caterina del Sasso Ballaro ★★★

Just south of Reno on the southeastern leg of Maggiore, beneath an inconspicuous car park in Piazza Cascine del Quiquio, an elevator descends to the magical hermitage of **Santa Caterina del Sasso Ballaro** (Via Santa Caterina 13, Leggiuno; www.santacaterinadel sasso.com; ℂ **0332-647-172**). Founded in the 13th century, this Dominican monastery sits photogenically against a sheer rock face, clinging to an escarpment 15m (49 ft.) above the lake. The serene complex of soft pink stone is embellished with Renaissance arches, a square bell tower, and pretty cobbled courtyards. Don't miss the 14th-century frescoes of biblical scenes in the chapel, which were hidden under lime during the Italian suppression of the monasteries in the 1770s and only rediscovered in 2003. The little gift shop sells honey, candles, and soaps made by the monks. Admission is free, but donations are accepted (open Apr–Oct 9am–noon and 2:30–6pm, Nov–Mar Sat–Sun 9am–noon and 2–5pm).

Where to Eat & Stay

There are many hotels scattered around Maggiore eager to grab the tourist dollar: some good, some bad, many indifferent. Here are two that are exceptional, at opposite ends of the price spectrum. Just like the hotels in the area, the standard of food can varies wildly; pick your restaurants in touristy Stresa with care.

Ristorante Piemontese ★★ NORTHERN ITALIAN   A cut above the myriad pasta/pizza places that haunt the town center, this is where all the Italian locals go to dine in Stresa. Here, the Bellossi family concentrates on producing serious cooking, offering excellent Barbera di Alba wines to round out your meal. Dishes such as porcini risotto and duck confit are proudly presented in elegant and romantic surroundings, with fish and game options changing according to season. Finish off with a cheeseboard of pungent local cheeses.

Via Mazzini 25, Stresa. www.ristorantepiemontese.com. ✆**0323-302-35.** Main courses 8€–20€. Tues–Sun 7:30–10:30pm. Closed Dec–Jan.

Ristorante Verbano ★★ SEAFOOD   Although many of the restaurants on the Isole Borromee are overpriced and underwhelming, Verbano is the exception (so you should probably book ahead on the weekends). For once on this touristy little island, the service is exemplary; you won't feel rushed and the waiting staff is courteous and informed. Not only is its position sublime, overlooking Isola Bella's Palazzo Borromeo (see p. 117) with lake waters lapping around the terrace—this would make a romantic proposal spot— but the food is pretty good, too. Chef Diego Pioletti specializes in cooking fish fresh from the lake as well as creating hearty homemade pasta dishes and traditional risottos; there's also a five-course gourmet menu option priced at 50€.

Via Ugo Ara 2, Isola Pescatori. www.hotelverbano.it. 𝄞 **0323-304-08.** Main courses 15€–30€. Daily noon–2:30pm and 7–10pm (winter closed Wed). Closed Jan.

Albergo Funivia ★★   This basic hotel up at the Poggia Sant'Elsa belvedere is only accessible by the Sasso del Ferro cable car (see p. 120). The upside—literally—is beautiful views over Lake Maggiore towards the Alps from the balconies in every room. It's best for summer visits when the weather can be almost guaranteed. The restaurant serves a simple local menu and the sun terrace is always crammed on sunny days. Little can beat sitting out there after dark and watching the lights around the lake glittering in the distance.

Via Tinelli, 15, Località Poggio Sant Elsa, Laveno Mombello. www.funiviedellagomaggiore.it. 𝄞 **0332-610-303.** 12 units. Doubles 80€. Unguarded parking at foot of funicular. **Amenities:** Bar; restaurant; Wi-Fi (free)

Grand Hotel des Iles Borromee ★★★   The vast, over-the-top Belle Epoque exterior of this majestic old hotel in Stresa faces Lake Maggiore with its manicured and landscaped gardens. The interior lives up to the exterior, too, and with panache; all is hushed, ornate, marble, and gilded, opulent as a mini-Versailles. Rooms vary from doubles with garden views, which are (relatively) staidly decorated with plush marble bathrooms, to the fabulously glitzy Hemingway Suite, which consists of three bedrooms, a living room, four bathrooms, and a terrace overlooking the lake—it's almost blinding in its marble, silk, stucco,

A swank suite at the Grand Hotel des Iles Borromee.

and gilt design. There's a blissful spa to chill out in and a gourmet restaurant with a lakeview terrace.

Corso Umberto I 67, Stresa. www.borromees.it. ⓒ **0323-938-938.** 172 units. 185€–450€ double; 400€–3,300€ suite (higher prices are summer rates). Rates include breakfast. Valet parking. **Amenities:** Restaurant; bar; concierge; spa; sauna; indoor pool; 2 outdoor pools; personal trainer; gym; helicopter pad; Wi-Fi (free).

9

LAKE GARDA
(LAGO DI
GARDA)

L ake Garda is the largest and eastern-most of the Northern Italian lakes, with its western flanks lapping against the flat plains of Lombardy and its southern extremes in the Veneto. In the north, its deep waters are backed by Alpine peaks. Garda's shores are green and fragrant with flowery gardens, groves of olives and lemons, and forests of pines and cypress.

Essentials

GETTING THERE Regular **trains** run from Milan Stazione Centrale and stop at Desenzano del Garda (fares start at 9.20€). From

> Sirmione: 130km (81 miles) E of Milan, 150km (93 miles) W of Venice; Riva del Garda: 170km (105 miles) NE of Milan, 199km (123 miles) NW of Venice, 43km (27 miles) S of Trent

here it's a 20-minute bus ride to Sirmione; buses make the short hop every half hour for 1.90€).

Hydrofoils and ferries operated by **Navigazione Laghi** (www.navlaghi.it; ✆ **800-551-801**) ply the waters of the lake. One to two hourly ferries connect Sirmione with Desenzano del Garda in season (20 min. by ferry, 3€); less frequently October to April.

Sirmione is just off the A4 between Milan and Venice. From Venice the trip takes about 1½ hours, and from Milan a little over an hour. There's ample parking in Piazzale Monte Baldo.

VISITOR INFORMATION **Sirmione**'s tourist office is at Viale Marconi 8 (www.comune.sirmione.bs.it;

PREVIOUS PAGE: **Biking along the shores of Lake Garda.**

Lemon groves are abundant around Lake Garda.

(𝒞 **030-374-8721**). There is also a tourism kiosk at Viale Marconi 2 just before the bridge into the old part of town. Hours vary depending on the season. In **Riva del Garda**, the tourist office is on the lakefront at Largo Medaglie d'Oro al Valor Militare 5 (www.gardatrentino.it/en, 𝒞 **0164-554-444**). Hours vary depending on the season. There's also a tourist office in **Gardone Riviera** at Corso Repubblica 8 (𝒞 **0365-20-347**).

Sirmione

Perched on a promontory swathed in cypress and olive groves on the southernmost edge of Lake Garda, photogenic Sirmione has been a popular spot since the Romans first discovered hot springs here. Despite the onslaught of summer visitors, this historic little town

Outdoor cafes dot the streets of Sirmione.

manages to retain its charm. Sirmione has lakeside promenades and pleasant beaches and is small enough for everywhere to be accessible on foot. It is chiefly famous for its thermal springs, castle, and northern Italy's largest Roman ruins.

Thermal baths in Sirmione.

The moated, fortified **Rocca Scaligero ★★★** (*©* **030-916-468**) was built on the peninsula's narrowest point and today dominates the *centro storico*. Built in the late 13th century by the Della Scala family, who ruled Verona and many of the lands surrounding the lake, the castle is worth a visit for its sweeping courtyards, turreted defence towers, dungeons, and views across Lake Garda from the battlements. It's open Tuesday to Saturday 8:30am to 7:30pm, and from 8:30am to 2pm on Sundays; admission is 4€, ages 18 to 25 2€.

From the castle, it's a 15-minute walk (or take the open-air tram from Piazza Piatti) along Via Vittorio Emanuele from the town center to the tip of Sirmione's peninsula and the **Grotte di Catullo ★★** (*©* **030-916-157**), romantically placed ruins with views across the lake. Built around A.D. 150, the remains are thought to represent two sizeable villas owned by aristocratic Roman families. A small museum of Roman artifacts found at the site includes jewelry and mosaic fragments (Piazzale Orti Manara 4; admission 6€ adults, 3€ 18–25; opening times vary, but are generally Apr–Sept

GETAWAY TO gardone RIVIERA

Halfway up the western shore of Lake Garda, this little resort—easily accessible by ferry or bus from Desenzano del Garda—offers visitors a gorgeous backdrop for a little relaxation. Oleanders dot the paved promenade, and the charming *centro storico* (Gardone Sopra) is filled with enticing bars and restaurants.

Uphill from Gardone Sopra, the **Heller Garden** (Via Roma 2; www.hellergarden. com; ☎ **0336-410-877**) is a tropical paradise founded by Arthur Hruska, a botanist who was also dentist to the ill-fated Tsar Nicholas II of Russia. Hruska planted this botanical haven in the 1900s, and 8,000 rare palms, orchids, and tree ferns now thrive here, thanks to the town's mild, sheltered climate. Today the gardens are curated by Austrian artist André Heller, whose sculptures can be found scattered among the water features, cacti, and bamboo copses. The garden is open March to October daily from 9am to 7pm; admission is 10€, 5€ for ages 6 to 11.

Gardone Riviera's other highlight is the **Vittoriale degli Italiani** (Via Vittoriale 12; www. vittoriale.it; ☎ **0365-296-511**),

the wildly ostentatious and bizarrely decorated villa home to Gabriele d'Annunzio, Italy's most notorious poet and sometime war hero. He bought this hillside estate in 1921 and died here in 1936; a visit pays tribute to d'Annunzio's hedonistic lifestyle rather than his fairly awful poetry. The claustrophobic rooms of this madcap mansion are stuffed with bric-a-brac and artifacts from his colorful life, including mementos of his long affair with actress Eleonora Duse. The patrol boat D'Annunzio commanded in World War I, a museum containing his biplane and photos, and the poet's pompous hilltop mausoleum are all found in the formal gardens that cascade down the hillside in luxuriant terraces. Summer concerts and plays are held at the amphitheater (www.anfiteatro delvittoriale.it). The villa is open daily; in summer from 8:30am to 8pm and winter from 9am to 5pm. Admission ranges from 8€ to 16€, depending on which parts of the estate you choose to visit. Note that villa tours are available in Italian only.

Tues–Sat 8:30am–7:30pm, Sun 9:30am–6:30pm; Mar–Oct Tues–Sat 9am–5pm, Sun 8:30am–2pm).

The massive amusement park **Gardaland** (www. gardaland.it; ☎ **045-6449-777**) is half an hour's drive east of Sirmione at Castelnuovo del Garda. This huge resort includes a hotel and an aquarium and is generally thronged during school vacation periods, but if Disneyland-type places are your thing, you may want to check it out.

Riva del Garda

The northernmost settlement on Lake Garda is a thriving Italian town, with medieval towers, a smattering of Renaissance churches and *palazzi,* and narrow cobblestone streets where everyday business proceeds in its alluring way. Note that Riva del Garda becomes a cultural oasis in July, when the town hosts the international **Largo di Garda Festival** of classical music (www.mrf-musicfestivals.com). Riva del Garda's **Old Town** is pleasant, although the only notable historic attractions are the 13th-century **Torre d'Apponale** in Piazza III Novembre, which is open in summer for visitors to climb its 165 steps for views across the lake, and the moated lakeside castle, **La Rocca.** Part of the castle now houses an unassuming civic museum with changing exhibitions (☎ **0464-573-869**; open daily 10am–12:30pm and 1:30–6pm, closed on Mon Oct–June; admission 3€ adults, 1.40€ ages 15–26 and over 65, children 14 and under free).

Where to Eat & Stay

Sirmione and Riva del Garda have a choice of pleasant, moderately priced hotels, all of which book up quickly

Riva del Garda.

in July and August, when the rates increase. The local cuisine features fish from the lake and plenty of pasta.

Osteria Al Torcol ★★ ITALIAN Consistently regarded as the stand-out restaurant in Sirmione, Torcol serves up good strong Italian cooking bursting with flavor, while managing to keep things moderately priced. This atmospheric place has an old-world wooden interior packed with bottles of local wines (many available by the glass) and a serving staff that really know what they are talking about. Signature dishes include fresh *tagliolini* (noodles) with pistachio and shrimp as well as a choice of fish of the day straight from the lake; it might be trout or pike. Book in advance if you want to eat outside on the rustic patio under the trees or at one of the lovely tables out front.

Via San Salvatore 30, Sirmione. ℰ **030-990-4605.** Main courses 13€–30€. Open May–Sept daily 12:30–3pm, 7:30–10:30pm; Oct–Jan Sat–Sun 12:30–3pm, 7:30–10:30pm; Feb–Apr Sat–Sun 7:30–10:30pm.

Trattoria Riolet ★ ITALIAN   As popular with Gardone locals as with summer visitors, the Riolet has unsurpassed views over Lake Garda from its hilltop aerie. Although the cuisine might be rustic—think pasta pesto, chicken kebabs cooked over the open fire and served with polenta, and lots of grilled fish—everything is freshly cooked and as fresh and tasty as could be. There's no menu, so take a leap of faith and follow your waiter's advice when ordering—and be sure to enjoy a carafe or two of the local wines.

Via Fasano Sopra 47, Gardone Riviera. ℂ **0365-205-45.** Thurs–Tues 7–10:30pm. Main courses 8€–25€.

Hotel du Lac et du Parc ★★★   Set in lush gardens, this massive, family-friendly resort has swimming pools, spas, and every conceivable luxury. Leading down to a little beach at the lake, the grounds are roomy enough to contain 33 bungalows and two luxurious blocks of apartments, still leaving ample space for the hotel. Somehow, despite the size of the operation, the service still feels personal and attention to detail is manifest everywhere. The gym, spas, and pools are spotless, the rooms are cheery and tasteful—ask for one overlooking the palm trees and rare plants of the park—and the breakfast buffet is five star. A tiny drawback is the over-fussy cuisine in the **La Capannina** restaurant, but there are plenty of dining options in Riva del Garda itself, a 15-minute walk away.

Via Rovereto 44, Riva del Garda. www.dulacetduparc.com. ℂ **0464-566-600.** 159 units in main hotel. 103€–229€ double; 170€–655€ suites. Rates include breakfast. Free parking. Closed Jan to mid-Apr. **Amenities:** 2 restaurants; 3 bars; 2 outdoor pools; indoor pool; gym; spa; sauna; gardens; babysitting; kids' club; water sports; concierge; room service; Wi-Fi (free).

out and about **ON LAKE GARDA**

Riva Del Garda's main attraction is the lake, lined with plush hotels and a waterside promenade that stretches for several miles past parks and pebbly beaches. The water is warm enough for swimming May to October, and air currents fanned by the mountains make Riva and neighboring Torbole the windsurfing capitals of Europe. Kitesurfing, kayaking, and sailing are all popular pastimes.

A convenient point of embarkation for a lake outing is the beach next to **La Rocca** castle (see p. 128), where you can rent rowboats or pedal boats for about 10€ per hour; from March through October, the concession is open daily 8am to 8pm.

Check out the sailing and windsurfing at **Sailing du Lac** at the luxurious **Hotel du Lac et du Parc** (see p. 132) where windsurf equipment can be rented for 47€ per day or 20€ for an hour. Lessons start at 49€ for 2 hours. Dinghy lessons are available from 75€ for 2 hours, rental from 25€ per hour. The school is open from mid-April to mid-October 8:30am to 6:30pm.

Lake Garda is also renowned for mountain biking; there are more than 80 routes around the waterside and up into the Alpine foothills. Rent bikes from **Happy Bike,** Viale Rovereto 72 (www.happy-bike.it; ℃ **34-7943-1208**), open daily 9am to 1pm and 3 to 7pm; rent a mountain bike for 14€ per day, or grab an eco-friendly electric bike for 49€ per day.

9

LAKE GARDA (LAGO DI GARDA) | Where to Eat & Stay

Hotel Eden ★ Once home of American poet Ezra Pound, this pink-stucco lakeside hotel is in the heart of the action in Sirmione, a stone's throw from the picturesque *centro storico*. Inside, the hotel is decked out in a bright and modern way with jazzy public spaces and vivid wallpaper designs; the breakfast room leads out to a shady terrace overlooking the lake, and a swimming pier juts out over the water. The modern take on a '70s theme is continued in the bedrooms, which have walls of splashy wallpaper enlivening the simple furnishings. Ask for a lakeview room as it can get a little noisy at night at the back of the hotel.

Piazza Carducci 19, Sirmione. www.hoteledensirmione.it. ✆ **030-916-481.** 30 units. 139€–183€ double. Rates include breakfast. Free parking nearby; 10€ in garage. Closed Nov–Easter. **Amenities:** Restaurant; bar; concierge; room service; Wi-Fi (free).

TURIN

10

t's often said that Turin is the most French city in Italy. The reason is partly historical and partly architectural. From the late 13th century until Italy's unification in 1861, Turin was the capital of the **House of Savoy.** These aristocrats of extraordinary wealth were as French as they were Italian, with estates that extended well into the present-day French regions of Savoy, the Côte d'Azur, and Sardinia. Under the Savoys, Francophile 17th- and 18th-century architects razed much of the original city and its Roman foundations, replacing them with broad avenues, airy piazzas, and grandiose buildings. As a result, Turin is one of Europe's great baroque cities, as befitting the capital (albeit briefly) of a nation.

Thanks in part to the 2006 Winter Olympics, and another makeover for

669km (415 miles) NW of Rome, 140km (87 miles) E of Milan

the 150th anniversary of Italian unification in 2011, Turin today has transformed itself from a former industrial power into a vibrant city full of museums, enticing cafes, beautiful squares, and designer stores. This elegant and sophisticated city is deservedly gaining a reputation as the go-to destination in northeast Italy.

PREVIOUS PAGE: **The cityscape of Turin backed by the Alps.**

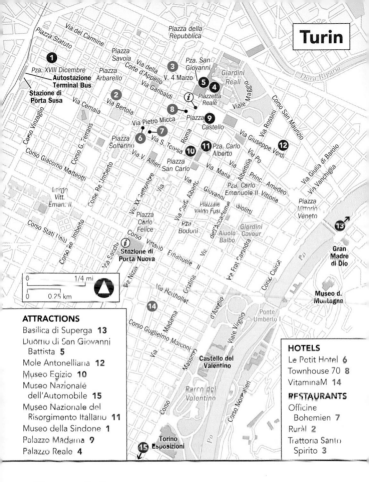

ATTRACTIONS

Basilica di Superga **13**
Duomo di San Giovanni
  Battista **5**
Mole Antonelliana **12**
Museo Egizio **10**
Museo Nazionale
  dell'Automobile **15**
Museo Nazionale del
  Risorgimento Italiano **11**
Museo della Sindone **1**
Palazzo Madama **9**
Palazzo Reale **4**

HOTELS

Le Petit Hotel **6**
Townhouse 70 **8**
VitaminaM **14**

RESTAURANTS

Officine
  Bohemien **7**
Rurài **2**
Trattoria Santo
  Spirito **3**

Essentials

GETTING THERE Domestic and international **flights** land at **Turin Airport** (www.aeroportoditorino.it; ℂ **011-567-6378**), about 13km (8 miles) northwest of Turin. Direct trains (www.gtt.to.it) run from the airport to GTT Dora Railway Station every 30 minutes between 5am and 11pm, costing 3€; the trip takes 19 minutes. SADEM (www.sadem.it) buses run between the airport and the city's main train stations, Porta Nuova and Porta Susa (40 min.; 6.50€). **Taxis** into town take about 30 minutes and cost 30€ to 50€, depending on the time of day.

Turin's main **train** station is **Stazione di Porta Nuova** on Piazza Carlo Felice. There is regular daily Trenitalia (www.trenitalia.com; ✆ **89-20-21**) service from Milan. The fastest trains take 1 hour, with fares averaging 29€ (check advance-purchase fares, however, which can be as low as 9€). Slower trains take up to 2 hours, with fares of 12.20€ to 17€. **Stazione di Porta Susa** connects Turin with local Piedmont towns and is the terminus for the TGV service to Paris; four trains a day make the trip to Paris in under 6 hours for around 98€, but there are often specials in the off-season for as low as 29€ each way.

Turin's main **bus terminal** is **Autostazione Bus,** Corso Vittorio Emanuele II 131 (www.autostazione torino.it). The ticket office is open daily 9am to 1pm and 3 to 7pm. Buses connect Turin to Courmayeur, Aosta, Milan, and many small towns in Piedmont. There is a 2-hour SADEM (www.sadem.it) bus service to Milan Malpensa Airport costing 22€.

Turin is at the hub of the autostrade network. The A4 connects Turin with Milan in 90 minutes. Journey time via the A5 to Aosta is also around 90 minutes.

GETTING AROUND   All the main sights of Turin are well within walking distance of each other. There's also a vast network of GTT trams and buses as well as one metro line (www.gtt.to.it; ✆ **011-57-641**). The Linea 7 tourist tram trundles around a circular route from Piazza Castello. Tickets on public transportation are available at newsstands for 1.50€ and are valid for

90 minutes. All-day tickets are 5€ and last 24 hours. There is no need to drive in the city center.

You can find taxis at stands in front of the train stations and around Piazza San Carlo and Piazza Castello. To call a taxi, you can dial **Pronto** at ✆ **011-5737**, but all hotel reception desks will order a taxi for you. Meters start at 3.50€ and prices increase by 1.25€ per kilometer; there are surcharges for waiting time, luggage, late-night travel, and Sunday journeys.

VISITOR INFORMATION The tourist office on the corner of Via Garibaldi and Piazza Castello (www.turismotorino.org; ✆ **011-535-181**), is open daily 9am to 6pm. There are also branches in **Stazione Porta Nuova** and at the airport (same phone; same hours).

The tourist offices on Piazza Castello and at Stazione Porta Nuova sell the bargain **Torino+Piemonte Card** for 26€. This is valid for one adult and one child up to age 12 for 48 hours and grants access to over 180 museums, monuments, castles, and royal palazzos, as

The ancient Roman gates in the Area Romano.

well as free public transport within Turin, plus discounts on car rentals, ski lifts, theme parks, concerts, and sporting events (3- and 5-day versions are also available). Check www.turismotorino.org/card for details.

CITY LAYOUT With the Alps as a backdrop to the north and the River Po threading through the city center, Turin has as its glamorous backbone the elegant arcaded **Via Roma**, lined with designer shops and grand cafes. Via Roma runs northwards through a series of ever-lovelier Baroque squares until it reaches **Piazza Castello** and the heart of the city around the palaces of the Savoy nobility.

From here, a walk west leads to the **Area Romano**, a mellow jumble of narrow streets that's the oldest part of the city. Its edge is marked by Via Garibaldi. Or turn east from Piazza Castello along Via Po to one of Italy's largest squares, the **Piazza Vittorio Veneto** and, at the end of this elegant expanse, the River Po and **Parco del Valentino.**

[FastFACTS] TURIN

ATMs/Banks
There are banks with multilingual ATMs all over the city center. Opening hours are roughly Monday to Friday 8:30am to 1:30pm and 2:30 to 4:30pm.

Business Hours
Stores are open Monday to Saturday from 9am–1pm and 4 to 7:30pm.

Consulates The consulates of the U.S., Canada, U.K., Australia, and New Zealand are in Milan (see p. 68).

Dentists Dr. Marco Capitanio at Via Treviso 24/G, (www.marco capitanio.com; ✆ **34-7157-8802**), speaks fluent English.

Doctors The Medical Center at Corso Einaudi, 18/A (www.medical-center.it; ✆ **011-591-388**) has some English-speaking staff.

Drugstores A convenient late-night pharmacy is **Farmacia Boniscontro,** Corso Vittorio

Emanuele 66 (📞 **011-538-271**); it is open all night but closes for lunch, 12:30 to 3pm, and is closed on Saturday and Sunday. The website **www.orari-di-apertura.it/farmacie-torino.htm** gives the opening hours of most of Turin's central pharmacies.

Emergencies

All emergency numbers are free. Call 📞 **112** for a **general emergency**; this connects to the **Carabinieri,** who will transfer your call as needed; for the **police,** dial 📞 **113;** for a **medical emergency** or an ambulance, call 📞 **110;** for the **fire department,** call 📞 **115.**

Hospitals

The **Ospedale Mauriziano Umberto I,** Largo Filippo Turati 62 (www.mauriziano.it; 📞 **011-508-1111**), offers a variety of medical services.

Internet

Many Turin cafes, bars, restaurants, and hotels now have Wi-Fi. Try, for example, **Busters Coffee** (www.busterscoffee.it) at Via Cesare Battisti 7/L near Piazza Castello and the University of Turin. This café offers free Wi-Fi and serves up Italian coffee, tea, American-style beverage concoctions, panini, and salads. Open Mon to Fri 7:30am to 7:30pm and Sat to Sun 8:30am to 7:30pm

Police

In an emergency, call 📞 **113;** this is a free call. The central police station (Questura Torino) is near Stazione di Porta Susa at Corso Vinzaglio 10 (📞 **011-558-81**).

Post Office

Turin's **main post office,** just west of Piazza San Carlo at Via Alfieri 10 (📞 **011-506-0265**), is open Monday to Friday 8:30am to 6.30pm and Saturday from 8:30am to noon. A list of central post offices and opening times can be found at www.quartieri.torino.it/ElencoPoste.asp.

Safety

Turin is a relatively safe city, but use the same precautions you would exercise in any large city. Specifically, avoid the riverside streets along the Po when the late-night crowds have gone home.

Exploring Turin

The stately arcades of **Via Roma,** Turin's premier shopping street, were designed in 1714 by Filippo Juvarra. This chic thoroughfare runs from the circular

Piazza San Carlo, Turin.

Piazza Carlo Felice, ringed with outdoor cafes and constructed around formal gardens, north into **Piazza San Carlo,** which is quite possibly Italy's most beautiful square. In summer Piazza San Carlo is Turin's harmonious outdoor *salone*, its arcaded sidewalks lined with big-name fashion stores and elegant cafes, including the genteel **Caffé Torino** (✆ **011-545-118**). In the center of the piazza prances a 19th-century equestrian statue of Duke Emanuele Filiberto of Savoy. A pair of 17th-century churches, **San Carlo** and **Santa Cristina**, face each other like bookends at the southern entrance to the square.

At the far north end of Via Roma, the **Piazza Castello** is dominated by **Palazzo Madama** (see p. 149), named for its 17th-century inhabitant, Christine Marie of France, who married into the Savoy dynasty in 1619. Further north still stands the massive complex of the **Palazzo Reale** (see p. 150), residence of the Savoy dukes from 1646 to 1865.

Duomo di San Giovanni Battista ★ CHURCH
One of the few pieces of Renaissance architecture in Baroque-dominated Turin, this otherwise uninspiring 15th-century cathedral tucked round the west flank of the Palazzo Reale is famous as the resting place of the **Turin Shroud** (see p. 145) when the shroud is not on display. The linen cloth is preserved in an aluminium casket specially manufactured by an Italian aerospace company in the temperature-controlled, air-conditioned **Cappella della Sacra Sindone** and closed off from human contamination with bulletproof glass. The shroud's casket is adorned with a crown of thorns; the faithful come in droves to worship at the chapel, which is the last one in the left-hand aisle. To learn all about the history of the shroud, head for the **Museo della Sindone** (see p. 148).

Piazza San Giovanni. www.visitatorino.com/duomo_torino.htm. ② **011-436-1540.** Free admission. Mon–Fri 7am–12.30pm, 3–7pm; Sat–Sun 8am–12:30pm, 3–7pm. Bus: 11, 12, 51, 55, 56, 61, 68. Trams: 4, 13, 15, 18.

Mole Antonelliana & Museo Nazionale del Cinema ★★★ MUSEUM   Turin's most peculiar building was once the tallest in Europe, begun in 1863 as a synagogue but then hijacked by the city fathers to become a monument to Italian unification (at the time, Italy was ruled by the House of Savoy from their power-base in Turin). The Mole has a squat brick base supporting several layers of pseudo-Greek columns, topped by a steep cone-like roof and a skinny spire, all of it rising 167m (548 ft.) above the streets. It is now home to Italy's National Film Museum.

The dramatic Museo Nazionale del Cinema.

The museum recently underwent a facelift to haul it into the digital age, adding interactive displays, mobile tagging, digital captions, and augmented reality features. Wi-Fi is now offered free inside the museum all the way up to the panoramic terrace. The first exhibits track the intriguing development of moving pictures, from shadow puppets to risqué peep shows and flickering images of galloping horses filmed by Eadweard Muybridge in 1878. The rest of the display uses clips, stills, posters, and props to illustrate the major aspects of movie production, from *The Empire Strikes Back* storyboards to the creepy steadycam work in *The Shining*. There are plenty of buttons to push and lots of interactive action to keep kids happy.

The highlight of a visit is the ascent through the roof of the museum's vast atrium and up 85 m (279 ft.) inside the tower to the 360-degree observation platform at the top, an experience that affords a stunning view of the gridlike streets of Turin and its backdrop of snowy Alpine peaks. At the end of a tour, a giant movie screen plays films on a loop outside the stylish Cabiria Café. Via Montebello 20. www.museocinema.it. ℭ **011-8138-511.** Museum and panoramic lift: admission 14€, 11€ seniors and students up to age 26, 8€ ages 6–18, free under 5. Museum only: admission 10€, 8€ seniors and students up to age 26, 3€ ages 6–18, free under 5. Panoramic lift only: 7€; 5€ students, seniors, and ages 6–18. Open Tues–Fri & Sun 9am–8pm, Sat 9am–11pm. Multilingual guided tours by advance booking. Bus: 18, 55, 56, 61, 68. Tram: 13, 15, 16

Museo Egizio (Egyptian Museum) ★★ MUSEUM

Turin's magnificent Egyptian collection is one of the world's largest—no surprise, since it was also the world's

History of the Turin Shroud

The Turin Shroud is allegedly the linen cloth in which Christ was wrapped when he was taken from the cross—and to which his image was miraculously affixed. The image on the cloth is of a bearded face—remarkably similar to the depiction of Christ in Byzantine icons—and a body marked with bloodstains consistent with a crown of thorns, a slash in the rib cage (made by the Roman centurion Longinus), what appear to be nail holes in the wrists and ankles, and scourge marks on the back from flagellation. Carbon dating results are confusing; some have suggested that the shroud was manufactured around the 13th or 14th centuries, while other tests imply that those results were affected by the fire that all but destroyed it in December 1532. Regardless of scientific skepticism, the shroud continues to entice hordes of the faithful to worship at its chapel in the Duomo di San Giovanni Battista and the mystery remains unsolved—just how was that haunting image impregnated onto the cloth?

first Egyptian museum, thanks to the Savoy kings and their explorers Bernardino Drovetti and Ernesto Schiaparelli, who voraciously amassed Egyptian ephemera until the early 20th century, when attitudes reversed against such cultural plundering. At the point of writing, this museum was a *lavoro in corso* (work in progress), as a flashy new museum was due to open any day. The collection contains artifacts squirreled together from all eras of ancient

The sarcophogus lid of Ibi at the Egyptian Museum.

Egypt, including a papyrus "Book of the Dead" and funerary objects. The most captivating exhibits are the exquisitely painted wooden sarcophagi and mummies of Kha and Merit, an aristocratic couple whose tomb was discovered in 1906, along with more than 500 funerary items. The new museum will feature an innovative system of escalators to lead visitors seemingly on a path along the Nile. There will also be a library, café, classrooms, and rooftop garden in the new four-level, 10,000-square-meter museum.

Via Accademia delle Scienze 6. www.museoegizio.it. (✆ **011-440-6903.** Admission 13€ adults, 9€ ages 15–18, 1€ ages 6–14, free for children 5 and under. Open Mon 9am–2pm, Tues–Sun 8:30am–7:30pm. Bus: 55, 56. Tram: 13.

Museo Nazionale dell'Automobile ★★★

MUSEUM   Not surprisingly in a city that spawned

Vintage cars at the Museo Nazionale dell'Automobile.

Fiat, the car is king at this whizzy, innovative museum. Alfa Romeos and lots of bright-red Ferraris feature heavily among the displays, which start with vintage cars from the days when road travel was only for the very wealthy and progress through to factory line car production for the masses. A note of social responsibility is struck by displays that highlight the social, financial, and environmental effects that combustion engines have had on the planet. More than anything, you get to gaze at gorgeous cars. You don't need to be a car buff to appreciate the lovely lines of a Maserati, and this is the perfect place to bring kids who have traipsed around one too many Baroque *palazzo*.

Corso Unità d'Italia 40. www.museoauto.it. © **011-677-666.** Admission 12€ adults, 8€ children 6–18 and seniors, free for children under 6. Open Mon 10am–2pm; Tues 2–7pm; Wed–Thurs, Sun 10am–7pm, Fri–Sat 10am–9pm. Metro: Lingotto.

Museo Nazionale del Risorgimento Italiano (National Museum of the Risorgimento) ★★★

MUSEUM   On the Piazza Carignano—one of the most majestic in a city full of splendid corners—the equally handsome redbrick *palazzo* of the same name acquired huge national importance as the sometime home of Italy's first king following the country's Unification in 1861. Originally built between 1679 and 1685 by Baroque maestro Guarino Guarini, the palace now houses the Museo del Risorgimento; at its heart is the ornate circular chamber where Italy's first parliament met. For an Italian museum, this is incredibly well organized, with clear, timed itineraries suggested in literature at the door as well as online. More than 30 artfully decorated rooms detail the military campaigns that led to Unification, both from an Italian and a European perspective; even non-Italians can easily appreciate the stirring drama of these years. Displays of uniforms, vivid warlike paintings, weapons, maps, and correspondence reveal feats of great derring-do as we are led through the Italy of the 19th century from Napoleon to Garibaldi. There's a refreshing amount of multilingual signage and labelling; this fascinating exhibition should be used as an example to some other Italian museums.

Via Accademia delle Scienze 5. www.museorisorgimento torino.it. ℂ **011-562-1147.** Admission 10€ adults, 8€ seniors, 5€ students; 4€ high-school students, 2.50€ primary school, free 6 and under. Tues–Sun 10am–6pm. Bus: 11, 12, 27, 51, 51/, 55, 56, 57. Tram: 13, 15.

Museo della Sindone (Holy Shroud Museum) ★★

MUSEUM   There are no Disneyesque special effects in this curiously endearing little museum, which is refreshing considering the Turin Shroud's hefty status as one of the world's most famous religious relics. A visit kicks off with a 15-minute film about the shroud, its provenance, and the various theories and mysteries surrounding it; then it's down to a series of rooms chronicling its history from the first firm mention in 1204, to the fire that nearly destroyed it in Chambéry in 1532, to its arrival in Turin with the House of Savoy

The Holy Shroud Museum.

in 1578, and the modern-day carbon-testing sagas. The tour finishes in the richly ornamented chapel of Santo Sudario, private place of worship for the Savoy dukes, where a copy of the shroud is displayed over the gleaming, gilded altar. The shroud itself is not displayed here (it is in the royal chapel of the Duomo, see above), and is only taken out periodically. Check www.sindone.org to find out when the shroud will next be displayed in the Duomo; advance reservations are usually required to see the shroud in its brief public displays.

Via San Domenico 28. www.sindone.it. ② **011-436-5832.** Admission 6€ adults, 5€ students, aged 12 and under, and seniors. Daily 9am–noon and 3–7pm.

Palazzo Madama—Museo Civico di Arte Antica (Civic Museum of Ancient Art) ★ MUSEUM

Looking like two buildings sandwiched together, Palazzo Madama dominates Piazza Castello; its medieval facade looks eastward, while the westward face is its

Baroque addition, created by the architect Filippo Juvarra in the 18th century, when he was giving Turin its elegant arcaded facelift. Once inside this massive structure, you'll discover it incorporates a Roman gate and tower; courtyards, apartments, and towers from the medieval castle; and several Renaissance additions. Juvarra also added a monumental marble staircase to the interior, most of which is given over to the all-encompassing collections of the Museo Civico di Arte Antica. The holdings cover four mammoth floors and focus on the medieval and Renaissance periods, which are shown off well against the castle's austere, stony medieval interior. On the top floor you'll find one of Italy's largest collections of ceramics, but it's all rather disorganized in layout. The star of the show here is Antonello da Messina's sublime "Portrait of a Man," hidden away in the Treasure Tower at the back of the building.

Piazza Castello. www.palazzomadamatorino.it. © **011-443-3501.** Admission 10€ adults, 8€ student and seniors, free under 18. Free admission for all on the first Tuesday of the month. Tues–Sat 10am–6pm; Sun 10am–7pm. Bus: 11, 12, 51, 55, 56, 61, 68; Trams: 4, 13, 15, 18.

Palazzo Reale (Royal Palace) & Armeria Reale (Royal Armory) ★ PALACE

Overshadowing the north side of the Piazza Castello, the residence of the House of Savoy was begun in 1646; the family lived here up until 1865. Designed by the architect Amedeo di Castellamonte, the palace reflects the ornately Baroque tastes of European ruling families of the time, while its sheer size gives some indication of the wealth of these medieval oligarchs. This Savoy palace gives the ostentatious frippery of Versailles a run for its money; there are throne rooms, dining rooms, ballrooms,

Impressive hardware on display at the Royal Armory.

bedrooms, Chinese rooms, and apartments hung with priceless Gobelins tapestries, all lavishly adorned with silk walls, sparkling chandeliers, ornate wooden floors, and delicate gilded furniture.

The east wing of the *palazzo* houses the **Armeria Reale,** one of the most important arms and armor collections in Europe, especially of weapons from the 16th and 17th centuries. It's also unusual for its collection of stuffed horses, which look ready to leap into battle at any moment.

Behind the palace are the formal **Giardini Reali (Royal Gardens),** laid out by André Le Nôtre, who designed the Tuileries in Paris and the gardens at Versailles.

The Savoy royal family had an even keener eye for paintings than for Baroque décor, amassing an impressive collection of 8,000 works of art. Currently awaiting a new home, the collection's highlights are on show in temporary accommodation in the **Galleria Sabauda** on the ground floor of the Palazzo Reale's

New Wing. (This is a few minutes' walk from the main *palazzo,* past the Duomo, see p. 143). The exhibition kicks off with early Piedmont and Dutch religious works works, plus a moody Rembrandt self-portrait and two massive paintings by van Dyck: "The Children of Charles I" (1637) and a magnificent equestrian portrait of Prince Thomas of Savoy (ca. 1634).

Now permanently housed n the basement beneath the Galleria Sabauda, the **Museo Archeologico** provides a thoughtfully designed exhibition, which tells the story of Turin's development from Roman through medieval times. Incorporated into the museum is a section of Roman wall, remnants from the theater nearby, and a mosaic only discovered in 1993.

The **Biblioteca Reale** (Royal Library) is also part of the Palazzo Reale complex; it's free to enter and you'll find it (eventually) on the right of the main entrance. Founded in 1831, its scholarly wooden interior houses 200,000 rare volumes as well as ancient maps and prints. On the opposite side of the gates is the fine **church of San Lorenzo,** designed by Baroque master-architect Guarino Guarini in 1666. Its plain facade belies the lacy dome and frothy interior.

Piazzetta Reale 1. www.ilpalazzorealeditorino.it. © **011-436-1455.** Palazzo and all exhibitions: admission 12€ adults, 6€ ages 18–25, free for children and seniors. Free admission for all on the first Sunday of the month. Tues–Sun 8:30am–7:30pm; last admission 6pm. Museo Archeologico closed Sun morning. Bus: 11, 12, 51, 55, 56, 61, 68; Trams: 4, 13, 15, 18.

Outlying Attractions

Basilica di Superga ★★ CHURCH   Half the fun of a visit to this lovely basilica is the 6.5km (4-mile) journey northeast of the city center on a narrow-gauge railway through the lush countryside of the Parco

The Basilica di Superga.

Naturale della Collina di Superga. The church was built as thanksgiving to the Virgin Mary for Turin's deliverance from the French siege of 1706. Prince Vittorio Amedeo II commissioned Filippo Juvarra, the Sicilian architect who designed much of Turin's elegant center, to build the magical Baroque confection on a hill high above the city. The eye-catching exterior, with its beautiful colonnaded portico, elaborate dome, and twin bell towers, is actually more visually appealing than the ornate but gloomy interior, a circular chamber ringed by six chapels. Many scions of the House of Savoy are buried here in the Crypt of Kings beneath the main chapel. Tours of the royal apartments are available in slots of 45 minutes, with a maximum of 15 people.

Strada della Basilica di Superga, 75, www.basilicadisuperga. com. ℰ **011-899-7456.** Basilica: free admission. Appartamento Reale: admission 5€, open summer Tues–Sun 9:30am–7pm, winter Sat–Sun 10am–6pm. Trains leave from Stazione

Sassi (4€ roundtrip) and stop at Piazza Gustavo Modena; from there, follow Corso Casale on east side of the River Po. Bus: 61 from side of Ponte Vittorio Emanuele I opposite Piazza Vittorio Veneto.

Palazzina di Caccia di Stupinigi ★ PALACE   Yet another Savoy family home is found at Stupinigi, just a few miles southwest from Turin. More great work commissioned in 1729 from the architect Filippo Juvarra resulted in a sumptuous, ornately decorated hunting lodge surrounded by royal forests. Built on a humungous scale, the palace's wings fan out from the main house, topped by a domed pavilion on which a large bronze stag is featured. Every bit as lavish as the apartments in the Savoys' city residence, Palazzo Reale (see p. 150), the interior is stuffed with furniture, paintings, and bric-à-brac assembled from their myriad residences, forming the **Museo d'Arte e Ammobiliamento (Museum of Art and Furniture).** Wander through the acres of apartments to understand why Napoleon chose this for his brief sojourn in Piedmont in 1805 while on his way to Milan to be crowned emperor. Outstanding among the many, many frescoes are the scenes of a deer hunt in the King's Apartment and the triumph of Diana in the grand salon. The elegant gardens and surrounding forests provide lovely terrain for a jaunt. At the time of writing, the palace is under extensive restoration, although still open to the public.

Piazza Principe Amedeo 7, Stupingi, Nichelino. www.ordine mauriziano.it/tesori.html. ℂ **011-358-1220**. Admission 12€, seniors 8€, children 6–14 5€. Tues–Fri 10am–5:30pm, Sat 10am–6:30pm. 8.5km (5¼ miles) southwest of the city center.

A Glimpse into Roman Turin

Close to Turin's Duomo (see p. 143) and partly incorporated into the Museo Archeologico (see p. 152) stand two landmarks of Roman Turin—the remains of a theater and fragments of wall, as well as the **Porta Palatina,** a Roman-era city gate, flanked by twin 16-sided towers on Piazza San Giovanni Battista. The **Area Romana** west of the Piazza Castello is the oldest part of the city, a charming web of streets occupied since ancient times.

Reggia di Venaria Reale ★★★ PALACE Completing the triumvirate of glitzy Savoy households around Turin, the Venaria was constructed in the mid–17th century to a design by Amedeo di Castellamonte, but sure enough Filippo Juvarra also had a hand in the design. This massive complex, its stables, and its awesome formal gardens are now on the UNESCO World Heritage Sites list. Reopened in 2011 after decades of work, Venaria now offers a great, family-oriented day out with loads of outdoor summer activities as well as a glimpse into the extraordinarily privileged lives of the Savoy family. The Fountain of the Stag dances to music in the lake outside the *palazzo*; in the grounds, there are follies aplenty and the mock-Roman Fountain of Hercules to discover. Permanent exhibitions in the house include the Peopling the Palaces lightshow conceived by film director Peter Greenaway, who also had a hand in the exhibitions at the Museum of Cinema (see p. 143) in Turin.

Piazza della Repubblica 4, Venaria Reale (10km/6¼ mi northwest of the city center). www.lavenaria.it. (© **011-499-2333**. Admission varies from 25€ for palace, gardens, and activities to 5€ for gardens only, with many price options in between. Tues–Fri 9am–5pm, Sat–Sun 9:30am–7:30pm (last admission 1 hour before closing). Bus: 11 from Piazza Repubblica. A Venaria Express bus runs Tues–Sun (40 min.), with stops at Stazione Porta Nuova, on Via XX Settembre, and at Stazione Porta Susa.

Organized Tours

Several tour companies run trips around Turin and Piedmont. **Viator** (www.viator.com; U.S. ✆ **702-648-5873**) offers an intriguing underground tour of the city's catacombs and hosts guided tours of the Barolo region (see p. 171). A hop-on, hop-off bus service circles the major attractions and is run by **Torino City Sightseeing** (www.torino.city-sightseeing.it; ✆ **011-535-181**), while **Delicious Italy** (www.delicious italy.com) showcases the food stores and restaurants that have given Turin its gourmet reputation.

Where to Stay

Turin has seen a recent injection of private capital into the hotel scene, and as a result, many boutique hotels have opened, giving travelers an alternative to the faceless frumpery of many of the city's older hotels.

Le Petit Hotel ★★ Unassuming from the front, the Petit Hotel has had a brush-up inside and offers very simple bedrooms with spotless, functional bathrooms. There's not much luxury but prices are very reasonable and the address is central. A casual restaurant offers pizza and pasta staples, though there are better places to eat within a couple minutes' walk. In summer the Marechiaro restaurant moves outdoors, offering a great spot for an early evening drink. The breakfast room has been upgraded and now offers a buffet of breads, cheeses, fruit, and pastries. The hotel also offers some smartly furnished self-catering apartments.

Via San Francesco d'Assisi 21. www.lepetithotel.it. ⓒ **011-561-2626.** 79 units. Doubles 89€–129€; apartments 150€–220€. Rates include breakfast. Free parking. **Amenities:** Restaurant; Wi-Fi 5€ for 3 hours.

Townhouse 70 ★★★   Part of a luxury chain that also has hotels in Milan, the Townhouse could not be better placed for sightseers, just steps away from Piazza Castello and the Palazzo Reale (see p. 150). It is a smooth, urbane hotel, with a tiny *aperitivo* bar tucked in one corner of reception and a breakfast room sporting one massive table, where smart businessmen and families all sit down together. Rooms are spacious for a city-center hotel, and decorated in soothing dark colors. The comfy beds have statement headboards; bathrooms have massive showers. The quieter bedrooms

Guests love the "piano table" in the living room of VitiminaM.

look over an internal courtyard, but keep in mind that there is a bit less privacy when your shutters are open. Via XX Settembre 70. www.townhouse.it. © **011-1970-0003.** 48 units. Doubles 112€–170€. Rates include breakfast. Parking in ZTL traffic-limited zone (fee). **Amenities:** Bar; concierge; room service (7–10am); Wi-Fi (free).

VitaminaM ★★★ This tiny B&B with just two rooms has a funky interior design full of arty offerings from up-and-coming Torino designers. The rooms are flooded with light, with silver and red color schemes, and the bathrooms are surprisingly luxurious, with full-length baths. Book well ahead as this is one of the hottest tickets in town; the only drawback is that the B&B is four floors up with no elevator. Via Belfiore 18. www.vitaminam.com. © **347-1526-130.** 2 units. 100€–120€ double. Rates include breakfast. Underground parking nearby 15€ per day. **Amenities:** Wi-Fi (free).

Where to Eat

Turin's gourmet reputation outshines other Italian cities renowned for their gastronomy. Many restaurants are strong advocates of the Slow Food movement, and even a cursory glance at a menu will tell you whether ingredients are local; look for porcini mushrooms and truffles in season. Wine lists should feature Barolo, Barbera, and Barbaresco reds and sparkling Asti whites. Turin is also home to the world's largest food and wine fair, the **Salone del Gusto** (www.salonedel gusto.it), which runs every two years in October.

Officine Bohemien ★★ PIEDMONT This offbeat, low-key restaurant down a side street resembles a St-Tropez cafe circa 1950s, with walls covered with black-and-white posters. It's casual and slightly edgy, run by a young, delightful staff. There's a laidback bar selling Piedmont wines and fancy cocktails while jazz plays in the background; frequent live-music events are held here. Lunch sees offerings of staple pasta dishes such as *spaghetti pomodoro e basilica* or big salads at really good prices; dinner is a little more sophisticated, with menus changing daily according to what's available. Great platters of grilled and smoked meats, regional cheeses, chutneys, and fruits and vegetables are all sourced locally; bread is made daily in the kitchens.

Via San Camillo de Lellis (was Via Mercanti) 19. www.officine bohemien.it. © **011-764-0368.** Main courses 8€–12€. Tues–Fri noon–3pm, 7:30–10:30pm; Sat 7.30–10:30pm.

Ruràl ★★★ MODERN PIEDMONT One to watch, Ruràl is an award-winning proponent of the Slow Food ethos (born in nearby Bra), with a menu that is currently taking Turin to the top of the gastronomic charts. Its deceptively simple white and blondwood interior strikes a classy note; the clientele is smart and the service friendly and informed. Chefs, under the auspices of Piero Bergese, emerge from the open-plan kitchen to discuss the dishes with customers. A great sharing plate of rabbit, "tonnato" (a creamy

---

Shaken, not Stirred

Turin gave the world the aperitif vermouth, which was invented in 1786 by Antonio Benedetto Carpano; the brands Martini and Cinzano are still made in the Piedmont region. Order a glass at the gorgeous **Art Nouveau Caffè** **Mulassano** at Piazza Castello 15 (www.caffemulassano. com; © **011-547-990**), or come early to enjoy coffee and tempting cannoli or dainty fruit tarts at the ornate marble counter.

---

sauce flavored with tuna) meats, veal sausage, carpaccio, and tartare showcases typical Piedmont specialties, and the wine list offers plenty of decent regional reds and whites. It's obvious that everybody involved in this project is obsessive about food and proud to present the best of Piedmontese rural gastronomy.

Via San Dalmazzo 16. www.ristoranterural.it. ✆ **011-2478-470.** Main courses 15€–30€. Tues–Sat 12:30pm–2:30pm and 7:30–11pm, Sun 12:30pm–2:30pm.

Trattoria Santo Spirito ★★ SEAFOOD In a bustling piazza a few minutes' walk from Palazzo Reale in the heart of the Area Romana, Santo Spirito is well loved for its vast platters of mussels, tuna carpaccio, simply grilled fish, and delicious fettucine served with lobster. Portions are huge, so don't be tempted to over-order, especially at lunchtime. It is testament to the standard of cooking here that this place has thrived since 1975 in a city where restaurants open and close every day; it's not haute cuisine but great rustic cooking with fresh ingredients and plenty of strong flavors. In summer, tables spread out onto the piazza; in winter there's a cozy fire inside and heaters warm the loggia.

Largo IV Marzo 11. www.trattoriaspiritosanto.com. ✆ **011-4360-877.** Daily 12:30–3:30pm, 7:30pm–midnight. Main courses 9€–25€, separate land and sea tasting menus available for 40€.

Outdoor Activities

Turin's beautiful playground is **Parco del Valentino,** which cradles the left bank of the River Po between the Ponte Umberto I and the Ponte Isabella. Its first incarnation was in 1630, when it was the private garden of the Savoy dukes, but the park was much

Rowers on the River Po, flowing through Turin.

extended in romantic English-landscape style in the 1860s and opened to the public. It's a romantic place to stroll among the botanical gardens, flowerbeds, and manicured lawns. The massive **Castello del Valentino**, built in 1660, was the pleasure palace of Christine Marie of France; it is closed to the public. The castle forms an incongruous backdrop to the **Borgo Medievale** (see p. 162), a riverside replica of a 15th-century Piedmontese village. It's a pleasant walk back into the city center along Corso Emanuele Vittorio II, or Tram 9 takes you back to Porta Nuova.

There are half a dozen rowing clubs on the Po; Reale Societa Canottieri Cerea (www.canottiericerea. it) is the oldest. Jogging and cycling routes follow the riverside pathways.

A little further afield, it takes around an hour to reach the hiking trails of the **Gran Paradiso** national park. Turin is also an hour away from the ski resorts of **Valle d'Aosta** (see p. 177) in the Alps, and it's just a little further to the sandy beaches of the **Riviera delle Palme** to the south.

Especially for Kids

There's plenty for kids to do in Turin. There are the open spaces of **Parco del Valentino** (see p. 160) to run around in, plus free admission to the open-air **Borgo Medievale,** a mock-Piedmontese village built for the Italian General Exposition in 1884 (Viale Virgilio 107; www.borgomedioevaletorino.it; ✆ **011-4431-701**; open 9am–7pm [8pm in summer]). Most young-sters will be intrigued by the **Museum of Cinema** at the Mole Antonelliana (see p. 143), or at least the trip up the Mole's tower to see the city lying far below.

The **Museo Nazionale dell'Automobile** pro-vides a modern antidote to Turin's baroque attractions, as does a trip south of the city center to the **Olympic sta-dium** (www.olympicstadiumturin.com), built for the 2006 winter games and now home to rival Serie A Italian football teams Torino and Juventus. Both the stadium and its sports museum are open for guided tours (Tues–Sun 2–6pm; tours 10€ adults, 8€ under 16, seniors, students).

And if all else fails, pop into **Caffè Fiorio** (Via Po 8; ✆ **011-8173-225**) for some delicious ice cream.

Shopping & Nightlife

Turin's high-end shopping area is quite simply one of the most beautiful in the world. The arcaded **Via Roma** does full justice to the exquisite fashions on sale in Gucci, Armani, Ferragamo, Max Mara, and so on. At the end of Via Roma, the glass-roofed **Galleria Subal-pina**, which links Piazza Castello with Piazza Carlo, competes with Milan's Galleria Vittorio Emanuele II for sheer opulence in its three levels of art galleries, anti-quarian bookstores, and cafes. For those whose pockets may not be quite so deep, **Via Garibaldi, Corso XX Settembre,** and the surrounding streets together offer mid-range international brands at reasonable prices.

Turin's famous chocolates.

The windows of Italian food shops are always a thing of joy, and the specialist delis and confectioners of Turin are no exceptions. **Confetteria Stratta** (Piazza San Carlo 191; ✆ **011-547-920**) and **Pasticceria Gerla** (Corso Vittorio Emanuele 11) are thronged daily for their extravagant pastries, cakes, and *gianduiotti* (chocolate with hazelnuts). Turin is famous for its quality confectionery—the city produces 40% of Italy's **chocolate** and celebrates it with its own festival, CioccolaTO (www.cioccola-to.it, dates change annually). Turin also has a branch of **Eataly**, the current top tip for gourmet Italian produce, at Via Nizza 230, a little out of the center in Lingotto.

Most newsagents in Turin have English language newspapers, and the two branches of **Feltrinelli** (Piazza Castello 19, ✆ **011-541-627** or Stazione Porta Nuova ✆ **011-563-981**) sell multilingual books.

Nightlife in the city that invented the vermouth *aperitivo* is sophisticated and, as in Milan, it starts in the cafes and bars and finishes very, very late. Squeeze in with the Torinese at the bar of **Caffè Platti** (Corso

The Markets of Turin

The **produce market** in and around Porta Palazzo takes over the gigantic Piazza della Republica Monday to Friday 8:30am to 1:30pm and Saturday until 6:30pm. A bustling **flea market** takes place in the warren of streets behind the Porta Palazzo every Saturday, among the antique shops on Via Borgo Dora. The second Sunday of every month, the same spot is the scene of an **antiques market,** the **Gran Balon** (www.balon.it), where more than 200 dealers from across northern Italy display their wares. Come December, a **Christmas market** sets out its stalls in Via Borgo Dora. Turin has many stores specializing in rare books and old prints, and these also sell their wares from stalls along the Via Po.

Vittorio Emanuele II 72; ☏ **011-506-9056**) for a vermouth, and pick from the plates of enticing little pizzas made on the premises. Choose a Slow Food restaurant for dinner, and then join models and footballers to dance at **Kogin's** (Corso Sicilia 6; ☏ **011-661-0546**). In summer, head for the Murazzi embankment along the River Po for live bands and DJs in late-night dance clubs.

Dance, opera, theater, and musical performances (mostly classical) are on the agenda all year around—check the website www.visitatorino.com—but September is the month to really enjoy classical music in Turin, when more than 60 classical concerts are staged around the city during the month-long **Settembre Musica** festival (www.mitosettembremusica.it; ☏ **011-442-4787**), which is hosted jointly with Milan. Beyond the festivals you'll find classical concerts at **Auditorium della RAI,** Via Rossini 15 (www.orchestrasinfonica.rai.it; ☏ **011-810-4653**) and dance performances, and operas staged at the city's venerable **Teatro Regio** (www.teatroregio.torino.it; ☏ **011-8815-241**; tickets at Piazza Castello 215).

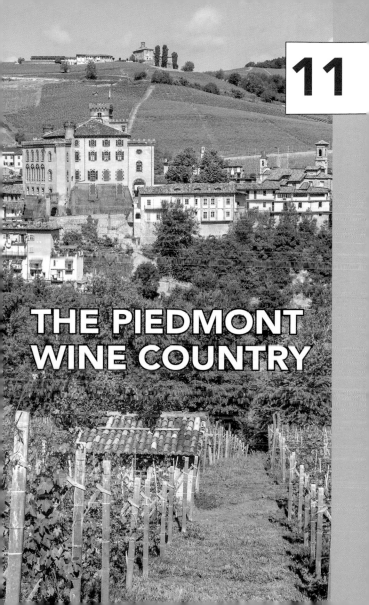

THE PIEDMONT WINE COUNTRY

South of Turin, the Po valley rises into the rolling hills of Langhe and Roero, flanked by orchards and vineyards. You'll recognize the region's place names from the labels of its first-rate wines, among them **Asti Spumanti, Barbaresco,** and **Barolo.** And vines are not all that flourish in this fertile soil—truffles top the list of the region's gastronomic delights, along with rabbit and game plus excellent cheeses.

Asti ★★★

Asti: 60km (37 miles) SE of Turin, 127km (79 miles) SW of Milan

The Asti of sparkling-wine fame is a bustling working city, but it has many treasures to uncover in its history-drenched *centro storico*—medieval towers (120 are still standing), Renaissance palaces, and piazzas provide the perfect setting in which to sample the town's most famous product, which flows readily in the local *enoteche* and cantinas.

ESSENTIALS

GETTING THERE Up to four **trains** per hour link Asti with **Turin Porta Nuova** (35 min; 5.25€) via **Trenitalia** (www.trenitalia.com; ✆ **89-20-21**). **Arfea** (www.arfea.it; ✆ **0131-225-180**) runs **buses** from Turin Autostazione to Asti; the trip takes 1 hour. By car, Asti can be reached in less than an hour from Turin via Autostrada 21.

PREVIOUS PAGE: **The town of Barolo, framed by vineyards.**

VISITOR INFORMATION The **APT tourist office** is near the train station at Corso Vittorio Alfieri 34 (✆ **0141-530-357**). It's open Monday to Saturday 9am to 1pm and 2:30 to 6:30pm; Sunday 9am to 1pm and 1:30pm to 5:30pm.

EXPLORING ASTI

Asti's historic heart is centered on three adjoining squares: **Piazza Libertá,** the vast **Campo del Palio,** and the grand arcaded **Piazza Alfieri.** Every year on the third Sunday of September, this area is mobbed for Asti's annual horse race, the **Palio** (www.palio.asti.it; ✆ **0141-399-482**), now held in Piazza Alfieri (originally it was in Campo del Palio). Like the similar race in the Tuscan city of Siena, Asti's Palio begins

Street performers at the Palio festival.

with a colorful medieval pageant through the town and ends with a wild bareback ride around the triangular Piazza Alfieri. First staged in 1273, the race coincides with Asti's other great festival, the **Douja d'Or** (www.doujador.it), a weeklong bacchanal celebrating the successful grape harvest.

Behind **Piazza Alfieri** stands the Romanesque-Gothic redbrick **Collegiata di San Secondo** (www.comune.asti.it; ✆ **0141-530-066;** daily 10:45am–noon, 3:30–5:30pm, Sun morning for Mass only). This church has two distinctions: it houses the Palio Astigiano, the prestigious banner awarded to the winning jockey at the Palio, and it also contains the tomb of St. Secondo, patron saint of both the horse race and the town. A Roman officer who converted to Christianity in A.D. 119, Secondo was martyred for his faith, beheaded in roughly the spot where his tomb now stands.

From Piazza Alfieri, the charming and largely pedestrianized **Corso Alfieri** bisects the old town and is lined with Renaissance *palazzi*. At the eastern end is the church of **San Pietro in Consavia** (© 0141-399-489; Tues–Sun 10am–1pm, 3–6pm, or until 7pm in summer) with a 10th-century Romanesque baptistery that was once a place of worship for the Knights of the Order of St. John. At the opposite, western extreme of Corso Alfieri you'll find the rotund **church of Santa Caterina,** abutting the medieval red-and-white brick-topped **Torre Rossa**.

Asti's 15th-century **Cattedrale di Santa Maria Assunta** (© 0141-592-924; daily 9am–noon, 3–6pm) is also at the western end of town in Piazza Cattedrale. Its austere exterior hides the gaudy excesses of the interior; every inch of the church is festooned with frescoes by late 15th-century artists, including Gandolfino d'Asti.

Being the agricultural and gourmet hotspot that it is, Asti is blessed with two **food markets.** The larger is held Wednesdays and Saturdays (7:30am–1pm) in the Campo del Palio and spills over into piazzas Della Libertà and Alfieri, with stalls selling cheeses, herbs, flowers, oils, and wines. The undercover **Mercato Coperto** on Piazza della Libertà is open daily except Sunday (Mon–Wed and Fri 8am–1pm, 3:30–7:30pm; Thur 8:30am–1pm; Sat 8am–7:30pm). Look for white truffles, *bagna cauda* (a fondue-like dip served warm and made with ingredients like olive, oil, butter, garlic, and anchovies), robiola cheeses, almond-flavored *amaretti* biscuits, and *nocciolata* (hazelnut and chocolate spread). The region's famous Asti Spumante DOCG sparkling wines can be bought from *cantinas* and *enoteche* in the town center and direct from some vineyards—a list is available from the **tourist office** at Corso Vittorio Alfieri 34 (see p. 169).

Visiting the Wine Villages

Gastro-destination **Alba ★★** (60km/37 miles south of Turin; 155km/96 miles southwest of Milan) is the jumping-off point for visiting the many vineyards of the Barolo wine-producing region. While it's a pleasure to walk along the Via Vittorio Emanuele and the narrow streets of the old town center, wine and food are what Alba's all about. Wherever you go, you'll end up peering into store windows to admire displays of wines, truffles, and the calorific but enticing *nocciolata* cake made of hazelnuts and chocolate. The streets are crammed with enough enticing restaurants to make gourmands very happy indeed.

Just to the south of Alba lie some of the Piedmont's most enchanting wine villages, sitting on hilltops among orderly rows of vines. The best way to see these villages is to drive; hire cars in Turin from **Avis,** Via Lessona Michele 30 (www.avis. com; ☎ **011-774-1962**), **Hertz,** at Corso Turati 37 (www.hertz.it; ☎ **011-502-080**), or **Sixt,** at Via Mongrando 48 (www.sixt.it;

Piedmont's signature wines.

© 011-888-768). Before you head out on the small country roads, provide yourself with a good map and a list of vineyards from the tourist office in Asti.

The main road through the wine region is the SS231, which runs between Alba and Asti. It is, however, a fast, busy, and unattractive highway; you'll want to turn off it to explore Piedmont's rustic backwaters among hazelnut groves and vineyards.

One such enchanting drive heads south from Alba to a string of wine villages in the **Langhe hills** (follow signs out of town for Barolo on the SP3). After 8km (5 miles), take the right turn for **Grinzane Cavour,** a hilltop village built around a castle harboring the **Enoteca Regionale Piemontese Cavour** (www.castellogrinzane.com; © 0173-262-159), which is open daily from 9am to 7pm (until 6pm Nov–Mar). Here you can enjoy a sampling of local wines from over 300 labels; the fine restaurant is perfect for lunch.

Retrace your route to the main road, turn left, and after another 4km (2½ miles) south, take the right fork to **La Morra,** another settlement perched among vineyards with panoramic views over the rolling, vineyard-clad countryside. There are several cafes and restaurants here in which to taste the local vintages. The **Cantina Comunale di La Morra** at Via Alberto 2 (www.cantinalamorra.com; © 0173-509-204) doubles as the tourist office and as a representative for local growers, selling Barolo, Nebbiolo, Barbera, and Dolcetto. It's open daily (except Tuesdays, when it's closed) 10am to 12:30pm and 2:30 to 6:30pm.

Barolo is a handsome little village dominated by two ancient castles; it's 5km (3 miles) along the SP58

The beautiful town of Barolo.

from La Morra. Here, too, you'll find a choice of restaurants and shops selling the world-renowned red wines from local vineyards. Among these outlets is the **Castello Falletti** (www.enotecadelbarolo.it; *C***0173-56-277**), revamped and reopened in May 2014 with a wine bar and an *enoteca* offering tastings in its cavernous cellars. A tasting includes three Barolo wines from different vineyards; costs are 5€ for three wines, 3€ for one. It's open Thursday to Tuesday 10am to 6pm.

Where to Eat & Stay

As well as a smattering of decent urban hotels, the Barolo region is the land of the *agriturismo*, with options to stay on wine estates in the hills of Langhe. Restaurants don't come much classier than the best-found in Piedmont.

Ristorante al Castello di Marc Lanteri ★★★

GOURMET Housed in the fairytale castle at Grinzane Cavour along with an *enoteca* selling the best of the region's wines, this renowned restaurant showcases the food of Michelin-starred chef Marc

Lanteri, who took over the kitchen in February 2015. Lanteri, a French chef born on the Italian border, considers his cuisine to be representative of Franco-Piedmont style. He makes everything from old standbys like *foie gras*, French onion soup, and traditional Piedmontese *bagna cauda*, to more modern and creative dishes like chestnut flour *pappardelle* or veal tartare with a Nebbiolo wine reduction. Try the "gusto & charme" menu (59€) for a series of small tastes of the chef's cuisine. The chef's American wife Amy serves as the restaurant's sommelier.

Via Castello 5, Grinzane Cavour. www.castellogrinzane.com. ℮ **338-700-1914.** Main courses 15€–20€. Mon 12:15–2pm, Wed–Sun noon–2pm, 7:30–10pm. Closed Jan.

Piedmont's Regional Wines

The wines of Piedmont are of exceptional quality and distinctive taste. They're usually made with grapes unique to the region, and grown on tiny family plots—making the countryside a lovely patchwork of vineyards and small farms.

Often called "the king of reds," **Barolo** is considered one of Italy's top wines, on par with Tuscany's Brunello and the Veneto region's Amarone. It is the richest and heartiest of the Piedmont wines, and the one most likely to accompany game or meat. **Barbaresco,** like

Barolo, is made exclusively from the red Nebbiolo grape, although it is less tannic. **Barbera d'Alba** is a smooth, rich red wine, the product of the delightful villages south of Alba (see p. 170). **Dolcetto** is dry, fruity, mellow, and not sweet, as its name leads many to assume. **Nebbiolo d'Alba** is rich, full, and dry.

As far as white wines go, **Spumanti** DOCGs are the sparkling wines that put Asti on the map. **Moscato d'Asti** is a delicious floral dessert wine, and the fiery local **Piedmont** *grappas* are none too shabby either.

Hotel Castello d'Asti ★★   Don't be put off by the slightly workaday street; this hotel is a find. Tucked into a lush courtyard garden near the *centro storico*, the Castello is in a historic townhouse with an elegantly updated interior. The beautifully appointed rooms are decorated in soft shades of black and cream with luscious marble bathrooms. The suites are more than spacious and all have their own balconies overlooking the gardens; there are also two luxurious self-catering apartments. Downstairs there's a lively bar and a sleek restaurant serving reliably good Piedmontese cuisine and offering more than 300 local wines.
Via G Testa 47, Asti. www.hotelcastelloasti.com. ☏ **0141-351-094.** 11 units. 125€–155€ double; 175€–235€ suite. Rates include breakfast. Free parking. Closed Jan. **Amenities:** Restaurant; bar; room service; Wi-Fi (free).

La Cascina del Monastero ★★★   Perfectly situated for exploring the Barolo wine region, this beautiful

La Cascina del Monastero is an ideal place for wine lovers to stay.

16th-century family-run estate is part laid-back B&B and part winery, all just minutes away from La Morra (see p. 171). Converted from an outbuilding of soft stone and arcading, the suites and apartments are beautifully furnished with exposed timbers, heavy Italian antiques, and brass bedframes. Exposed walls, beams, and wooden floors add to the traditional ambience of the place, while the bathrooms have every modern convenience. Guest facilities include an unusual spa, which has a sauna in what appears to be a massive wine barrel; a sun terrace; and, best of all, the chance to taste the wines produced on the estate. There's no restaurant (there are plenty of choices nearby), but the breakfast buffet kicks off the day in fine style. A camping area is available amid lovely scenery near the main house.

Cascina Luciani 112A, Frazione Annunziata, La Morra. www. cascinadelmonastero.it. *0173-509-245.* 10 units. 115€–125€ double; 125€–135€ apt. Rates include breakfast. Free parking. Closed Jan and sometimes Feb. **Amenities:** Children's playground; spa; outdoor pool; room service; sauna; Wi-Fi (free).

Palazzo Finati ★★

Hidden away behind a fine *palazzo* facade within easy reach of Alba's gourmet restaurants, the Finati offers a choice of individually designed rooms, some with frescoed ceilings and terraces overlooking the

A suite at Palazzo Finati.

inner courtyard, and all offering a taste of old-fashioned luxury. Rooms can be connected for family stays. The breakfast buffet includes fresh pastries, fruit, local cheeses, and cured hams, all served in a brick-ceilinged, barrel-vaulted dining room.

Via Vernazza 8, Alba. www.palazzofinati.it. ℭ **0173-366-324.** 9 units. 150€–180€ double, 179€–240€ suite. Rates include breakfast. Parking 10€–15€ per day (request in advance). **Amenities:** Wi-Fi (free).

AOSTA &
VALLE D'AOSTA

T ucked up against the French and Swiss borders in northwest Italy, the Aosta Valley is a land of harsh, snow-capped peaks, lush pastures, thick forests, waterfalls cascading into mountain streams, and romantic castles clinging to wooded hillsides. A year-round stream of skiers, hikers, cyclists, and nature lovers flock to this tiny Alpine region north of Turin for the scenery, outdoor adventure, and rustic gastronomy.

Aosta
ESSENTIALS

GETTING THERE Aosta is served by 20 **trains** a day to and from **Turin** (2 hr.,

> Aosta: 113km (70 miles) N of Turin, 184km (114 miles) NW of Milan; Courmayeur-Entrèves: 35km (22 miles) W of Aosta, 148km (92 miles) NW of Turin

change in Ivrea or Chivasso; tickets 9.45€) aboard **Trenitalia** (www.trenitalia.com; © **89-20-21**). Bus service to Aosta is much less handy: There are only a couple of direct buses from Turin Porta Nuova per day (most change in Ivrea), and even the direct trip takes 2 hours, the indirect route more than 3. However, a SAVDA bus conveniently connects Aosta hourly to **Courmayeur** (1 hr., 3.50€) and other popular spots in the valley.

Autostrada A5 from Turin shoots up the length of Valle d'Aosta en route to France and Switzerland via the Mont Blanc tunnel; there are numerous exits in the valley. The trip from Turin to Aosta normally takes about 90

PREVIOUS PAGE: **Skiing near Courmayeur.**

minutes, but traffic can be heavy on weekends in the ski season.

VISITOR INFORMATION   The **tourist office** in Aosta (Piazza Porta Praetoria 3; www.lovevda.it; ✆ **0165-236-627**) dispenses a wealth of information on hiking trails, ski lifts and passes, bike rentals, and rafting trips. It's open daily 9am to 7pm.

EXPLORING AOSTA

An appealing mountain town with an ancient heart, Aosta—nicknamed "the Rome of the Alps"—is surrounded by snowcapped peaks and steeped in a history that goes back to Roman times. Although you're not going to find much pristine Alpine quaintness here in the Valle d'Aosta's busy tourist center, you will find Roman ruins, medieval bell towers, and chic shops. Aosta's **weekly market** day is Tuesday, when stalls selling food, clothes, and crafts fill the Piazza Cavalieri di Vittorio Veneto.

Well-preserved city walls date from the days when Aosta was one of Rome's most important trading and military outposts. A **Roman bridge** spans the River Buthier and two Roman gates arch gracefully across the Via San Anselmo. The **Porta Pretoria** forms the western entrance to the Roman town and the **Arco di Augusto** the eastern entrance. The **Teatro Romano** and the ruins of the **amphitheater** are north of the Porta Pretoria; the ruins of the **forum** are in an adjacent park. The theater and

The Funivia skyway up Monte Bianco (Mont Blanc).

forum are open generally from 9am–6pm, typically closed for a few hours in the afternoon in the winter, and admission is free. Architectural fragments from these monuments that were found during excavations are displayed in Aosta's **Archaeological Museum** at Piazza Roncas 12 (© **0165-275-902;** free admission; Tues-Sun 10am–1pm, 2pm–6pm).

The Valle d'Aosta

Most visitors to the Valle d'Aosta come here for the outdoor activities rather than to sightsee; the region has some of Italy's best hiking trails. In summer climbers, cyclists, and ramblers head for the untamed **Parco Nazionale del Gran Paradiso** (see "Italian Wilderness," p. 183). In winter, the meadows and alpine forests around **Cogne** boast some of the region's best cross-country skiing. There's an **ice rink** in Aosta

Hiking the Valle d'Aosta.

called Art on Ice at Corso Lancieri di Aosta 47 (© **0165-185-7281**), and if you're after something a bit different, consider **dog sledding** (www.dogsled man.com/index.php) near Courmayeur.

However, most visitors come for the **downhill ski-ing** and snowboarding destinations of **Courmayeur, Breuil-Cervinia**, and the **Monte Rose** ski area around the resort towns of Champoluc and Gressoney. There are trails for all levels, from gentle nursery slopes to black runs and mogul fields. Expert skiers are best off at high-altitude **La Thuile** for excellent off-trail powder and heli skiing. The ski season kicks off in early December and, weather permitting, runs through April. Altogether there are 800km (500 miles) of ski runs available under the **Valle d'Aosta ski pass**; multi-day passes cost from 133€ for 3 days up to 485€ for 2 weeks. One child under age 8 skis free with each adult that buys the pass. More details are avail-able at www.skivallee.it.

Where to Eat & Stay

In the ski season, many hotels in Valle d'Aosta expect guests to eat on the premises and stay 3 nights or more, but outside busy tourist times, they are more flexible.

The Valle d'Aosta is the land of mountain food—hams and salamis, creamy polenta—and buttery Fon-tina is the cheese of choice.

Osteria da Nando ★★ FONDUE   This cheery terracotta-colored *osteria* is a true family affair, run under the beady eye of Germana Scarpa, who has been the boss here since 1957. Since then it has become one of Aosta's most popular restaurants for its

Osteria da Nando has been family run since 1957.

fondues in many guises, from bourguignonne served with tender beef fillet to *raclette* served with creamy Fontina cheese and chunks of chewy bread, alongside the archetypal Piedmontese dish of *bagna cauda* (anchovy fondue). Desserts are a little basic, French-style crèpes and gateaux, but the wine selection is impressively local.

Via Sant'Anselmo 99. www.osterianando.com. ✆ **0165-44-455.** Main courses 12€–25€. Daily (except closed Tues) noon–2pm, 7:30–10pm. Closed 2 weeks late June to early July.

Ristorante La Palud ★★ PIZZA/SEAFOOD There are Monte Bianco and glacier views from this buzzing pizzeria, and due to its position near the tunnel into France, it is nearly always packed. With the opening of the new cable-car service, reservations are recommended. It's popular for its deliciously crispy pizzas, creamy polenta dishes, and fresh fish brought up from the Ligurian coast. In summer sit outside on the

Italian Wilderness

The little town of Cogne is the gateway to one of Europe's finest parcels of unspoiled wilderness, **Parco Nazionale del Gran Paradiso.** Once the hunting grounds of King Vittorio Emanuele II, this vast and lovely national park—Italy's oldest—encompasses the jagged peaks of **Gran Paradiso** (4,061 m/13,323-ft. high), five valleys, and a total of 703 sq. km (271 sq. miles) of forests and pastureland. Many Alpine beasts roam wild here, including the ibex (curly-horned goat) and the elusive chamois (small antelope), both of which are nearly extinct in Europe. Humans can roam these wilds via a vast network of well-marked **hiking trails**. As well as being a hikers' paradise, Cogne is also well respected for its 80km (50 miles) of challenging cross-country (Nordic) skiing trails; check www.funiviegranparadiso.it for more. The park's main **visitor center** is at Via Alpetta, Ronco Canavese (www.pngp.it/en; ☏ **011-860-6233**). Admission is free.

flower-filled terrace; in winter huddle around the open fire and admire the drifts of snow piled up outside. Strada la Palud 17, Courmayeur. www.lapalud.it. ☏ **0165-89-169.** Main courses 10€–25€. Mon–Sun noon–3:30pm, 7:30–10:30pm.

Hostellerie du Cheval Blanc ★★ Traditional wooden chalet this is not, but if you're after family comforts and town-center convenience plus Alpine views and a garden, the modern design of the Cheval Blanc (white cow) fits the bill. The hotel is designed around a massive atrium with stylish leather sofas and has two restaurants; Le Petit is fairly expensive, but the Brasserie lends itself to early suppers with kids. The rooms are conventionally decorated in muted shades, and the bathrooms come in highly ornate marble, most with baths as well as showers. For skiers, a winter shuttle runs to the cable car up to Pila, while the pool and sauna provide perfect après-ski relaxation before a night of R&R in the bars of Aosta.

Rue Clavalité 20, Aosta. www.chevalblanc.it. ℂ **0165-239-140.** 55 units. 120€ doubles; 160€–180€ suite. Rates include breakfast. Free parking. **Amenities:** 2 restaurants; bar; children's playroom; indoor pool; gym; sauna; spa; room service; Wi-Fi (free).

13

PLANNING

taly is loaded with "must see" cities and sights, and most of us have limited vacation time. You want to get there efficiently, get around by road or rail without hassle, and spend as much time soaking up the atmosphere of *Bella Italia* as you can. This chapter shows you how. It may be a long way from home, but when you get there Italy need not be expensive: Below you'll find advice on where and how to shave travel costs without trimming your fun. (And for the best budget accommodations when you get there, see this guide's individual chapters.) Want some more good news? Recent changes in the exchange rate have made Italy cheaper to visit now than any time in at least a decade.

GETTING THERE
By Plane

If you're flying across an ocean, you'll most likely land at **Milan Malpensa** (MXP; www.milanomalpensa-airport.com), 45km (28 miles) northwest of central Milan's much smaller (CIA; www.adr.it/ciampino) serves low-cost airlines connecting to European cities and other destinations in Italy. LIN; www.milan olinate-airport.com). For information on getting to central Milan, see p. 62.

PREVIOUS PAGE: **Admiring the inside of the Duomo in Milan.**

Several services connect Bergamo's airport with Milan's Stazione Centrale, including **Orioshuttle** (www.orioshuttle.com; ☏ **035-330-706**). The service runs approximately half-hourly all day, a little less frequently on weekends. Journey time is 50 minutes. Tickets cost from 4€ if you book online ahead of time.

Begin thinking about flying plans at least 6 months ahead of time. Consider exchange rate movements: Fares may be calculated in US dollars or euros, depending on the airline. The key window for finding a **deal** is usually between 5 and 6 months ahead of your departure according to a massive study of some 21 million fare transactions by the Airline Reporting Corporation (a middleman between travel agencies and the airlines). They also found that those who booked on a Sunday statistically found the best rates (on average they paid 19% less than those who booked midweek). Run searches through the regular online agents such as Expedia, as well as metasearch engines like **DoHop.com, Kayak.com, Skyscanner.net,** and **Momondo.com**. For complex journeys, with multiple departures, doing multiple searches (so affordable intra European airlines such as Germanwings, Easy Jet and Ryanair show up on the search) is a good way to find deals; a specialist flight agent such as **RoundtheWorldFlights.com** or **AirTreks.com** will also likely save you money.

By Train

Italy's major cities are well connected to Europe's rail hubs. You can arrive in Milan on direct trains from France (Nice, Paris, Lyon) by TGV, or from Switzerland, and connect from there to Venice or Florence or Rome (see "Getting Around," p. 193). Direct trains from central and Eastern Europe arrive at Verona and Venice. TGV services connect France with Turin.

Thello (www.thello.com) also operates an overnight service connecting Paris with Milan and Venice. After crossing the Alps in the dead of night, the train calls at Milan, Brescia, Verona, Vicenza, and Padua, before arriving in Venice around 9:30am. For Florence, Rome, and points south, alight at Milan (around 6am) and switch to Italy's national high-speed rail lines; see below. Accommodation on the Thello train is in sleeping cars, as well as in six- and four-berth couchettes. Prices range from 35€ per person for the cheapest fare in a six-berth couchette to 290€ for sole occupancy of a sleeping car. It's worth paying the extra for private accommodations if you can.

Book in advance online or with **Rail Europe** (www.raileurope.com; ℂ **800-622-8600**) or **International Rail** (www.internationalrail.com; ℂ **+44-871-231-0790**).

GETTING AROUND
By Car

Much of Italy is accessible by public transportation, but to explore vineyards, countryside, and smaller towns, a car will save you time. You'll get the **best rental rate** if you book your car far ahead of arrival. Try such websites as **Kayak.com**, **CarRentals.co.uk**, **Skyscanner.net**, and **Momondo.com** to compare prices across multiple rental companies and agents. Car rental search companies usually report the lowest rates being available between 6 and 8 weeks ahead of arrival. Rent the smallest car possible and request a **diesel** rather than a petrol engine, to minimize fuel costs.

You must be 25 or older to rent from many agencies (although some accept ages 21 and up, at a premium price).

The legalities and contractual obligations of renting a car in Italy (where accident rates are high) are more complicated than those in almost any other country in Europe. You also must have nerves of steel, a sense of humor, and a valid driver's license or **International Driver's Permit.** Insurance on all vehicles is compulsory.

Note: If you're planning to rent a car in Italy during high season, you should **book well in advance.** It's not unusual to arrive at the airport in Milan in June or July to find that every agent is all out of cars, perhaps for the whole week.

It can sometimes be tricky to get to the *autostrada* (fast highway) from the city center or airport, so consider renting or bringing a GPS-enabled device, or installing an offline sat-nav app on your phone. In bigger cities you will first have to get to the *tangenziale,* or beltway, which will eventually lead to your highway of choice.

The going can be slow almost anywhere, especially on Friday afternoons leaving the cities and Sunday nights on the way back into town, and rush hour around the cities any day of the week can be epic. Driving for a day or so either side of the busy *ferragosto* (August 15) holiday is to be avoided *at all costs.* See **www.autostrade.it** for live traffic updates and a road-toll calculator.

Autostrada tolls can get expensive, costing approximately 1€ for every 15km (10 miles), which means that it costs about 18€ for a trip from Rome to Florence. Add in the high price of fuel (averaging over 1.50€ *per liter* at time of writing) and car rental, and it's often cheaper to take the train, even for two people.

Before leaving home, you can apply for an **International Driving Permit** from the American Automobile Association (www.aaa.com; ✆ **800/622-7070** or 650/294-7400). In Canada, the permit's available from the Canadian Automobile Association (www.caa.ca; ✆ **416/221-4300**). Technically, you need this permit and your actual driver's license to drive in Italy, though in practice your license itself often suffices. Visitors from within the EU need only take their domestic driver's license.

Italy's equivalent of AAA is the **Automobile Club d'Italia (ACI**; www.aci.it). They're the people who respond when you place an emergency call to ✆ **803-116** (✆ 800-116-800 from a non-Italian cellphone) for road breakdowns, though they do charge for this service if you're not a member.

DRIVING RULES   Italian drivers aren't maniacs; they only appear to be. Spend any time on a highway and you will have the experience of somebody driving up insanely close from behind, headlights flashing. Take a deep breath and don't panic: This is the aggressive signal for you to move to the right so he (invariably, it's a "he") can pass, and until you do he will stay mind-bogglingly close. On a two-lane road, the idiot passing someone in the opposing traffic who has swerved into your lane expects you to veer obligingly over toward the shoulder so three lanes of traffic can fit—he would do the same for you. Probably. Many Italians seem to think that blinkers are optional, so be aware that the car in front could be getting ready to turn at any moment.

Autostrade are toll highways, denoted by green signs and a number prefaced with an *A,* like the A1 from Milan to Florence, Rome, and Naples. A few fast highways aren't numbered and are simply called a *raccordo,* a connecting road between two cities (such as Florence–Siena and Florence–Pisa).

Strade statali (singular is *strada statale*) are state roads, sometimes without a center divider and two lanes wide (although sometimes they can be a divided four-way highway), indicated by blue signs. Their route numbers are prefaced with an *SS,* as in the SS11 from Milan to Venice. On signs, however, these official route numbers are used infrequently. Usually, you'll just see blue signs listing destinations by name with arrows pointing off in the appropriate directions. The *strade statali* can be frustratingly slow due to traffic, traffic lights, and the fact that they bisect countless towns: When available, pay for the autostrada.

The **speed limit** on roads in built-up areas around towns and cities is 50 kmph (31 mph). On two-lane roads it's 90 kmph (56 mph) and on the highway its 130 kmph (81 mph). Italians have an astounding disregard for these limits. However, police can ticket you and collect the fine on the spot. The blood-alcohol limit in Italy is .05%, often achieved with just two small drinks; driving above the limit can result in a fine of up to 6,000€, a driving ban, or imprisonment. The blood alcohol limit is set at zero for anyone who has held a driver's license for under 3 years.

Safety belts are obligatory in both the front and the back seats; ditto child seats or special restraints for minors under 1.5 meters (5 ft.) in height, though this latter regulation is often ignored. Drivers may not use a handheld cellphone while driving—yet another law that locals seem to consider optional.

PARKING   On streets, **white lines** indicate free public spaces, **blue lines** are pay public spaces, and **yellow lines** mean only residents are allowed to park. Meters don't line the sidewalk; rather, there's one machine on the block where you punch in coins corresponding to how long you want to park. The machine spits out a ticket that you leave on your dashboard.

If you park in an area marked *parcheggio disco orario,* root around in your rental car's glove compartment for a cardboard parking disc (or buy one at a gas station). With this device, you dial up the hour of your arrival and display it on your dashboard. You're allowed *un'ora* (1 hr.) or *due ore* (2 hr.), according to the sign. If you do not have a disk, write your arrival time clearly on a sheet of paper and leave it on the dash.

Parking lots have ticket dispensers, but exit booths are not usually manned. When you return to the lot to depart, first visit the office or automated payment machine to exchange your ticket for a paid receipt or token, which you will then use to get through the exit gate.

ROAD SIGNS   A **speed limit** sign is a black number inside a red circle on a white background. The **end of a speed zone** is just black and white, with a black slash through the number. A red circle with a white background, a black arrow pointing down, and a red arrow pointing up means **yield to oncoming traffic,** while a point-down red-and-white triangle means **yield ahead.**

Many city centers are closed to traffic and a simple white circle with a red border, or the words *zona pedonale* or *zona traffico limitato*, denotes a **pedestrian zone** (you sometimes drive through to drop off baggage at your hotel); a white arrow on a blue background is used for Italy's many **one-way streets;** a mostly red circle with a horizontal white slash means **do not enter.** Any image in black on a white background surrounded by a red circle means that image is **not allowed** (for instance, if the image is two cars next to each other, it means no passing; a motorcycle means no Harleys permitted; and so on). A circular sign in blue with a red circle-slash means **no parking.**

Gasoline (gas or petrol), *benzina*, can be found in pull-in gas stations along major roads and on the outskirts of town, as well as in 24-hour stations along the autostrada. Almost all stations are closed for the *riposo* and on Sundays (except for those on the autostrade), but the majority of them have a machine that accepts cash. Unleaded gas is *senza piombo*. Diesel is *gasolio*.

By Train

Italy, especially the northern half, has one of the best train systems in Europe with most destinations connected. The train is an excellent option if you're looking to visit the major sites without the hassle of driving. The vast majority of lines are run by the state-owned **Ferrovie dello Stato,** or FS (www.trenitalia.com; ✆ **89-20-21**). A private operator, **Italo** (www.italo treno.it; ✆ **06-07-08**) operates on the Turin–Milan–Florence–Rome–Naples–Salerno high-speed line, and the branch from Bologna northward to Padua and Venice.

Travel durations and the prices of the tickets vary considerably depending on what type of train you are traveling on. The country's principal north–south high-speed line links Turin and Milan to Bologna, Florence, Rome, Naples, and Salerno. Milan to Rome, for example, takes under 3 hours on the quick train, and costs 86€ if you want to travel on the spot, though you can find tickets as low as 20€ if you buy ahead and travel in off-peak hours. If you want to bag the cheapest fares on high-speed trains, aim to **book around 100 to 120 days before your travel dates.** You can do everything online. Both Italo and the state railway operate a ticketless system: Just show your confirmation email (which has a unique PNR code).

Types of Trains   The speed, cleanliness, and overall quality of Italian trains vary. **High-speed trains** usually have four classes: Standard, Premium, Business, and Executive on the state railway; Smart, eXtra Large, First, and Club Executive on Italo. The cheapest of these, on both operators, is perfectly comfortable, even on long legs of a journey. These are Italy's premium rail services. The **Frecciarossa** and **Italo** trains are the nicest of the nice and the fastest of the fast (Italy's bullet train). They operate on the Turin–Milan–Florence–Rome–Naples line, and run up to 300 kmph (186 mph). The **Frecciargento** uses similar hardware, but goes a bit slower; it links Naples, Rome, Florence, Verona, and Venice at speeds of up to 250 kmph (155 mph). With a maximum speed of 200 kmph (124 mph), the **Frecciabianca** links Milan and Turin with Venice and cities down the Adriatic coastline as far as Italy's heel. They are all generically called

Le Frecce. Speed and cleanliness come at a price, with tickets for the high-speed trains usually costing around three times as much as a slower "regional" train. On high-speed services you **must make a seat reservation** when you buy a ticket. If you are traveling with a rail pass (see p. 197), you must pay a 10€ supplementary fee to ride them and reserve a seat. Passes are not valid (yet) on Italo.

Intercity (IC) trains are one step down, both in speed and in comfort, but are a valid option that also requires a seat reservation. The slower **Regionale (R)** and **Regionale Veloce (RV)** make many stops. Old *Regionale* rolling stock is slowly being replaced, but they can still sometimes be on the grimy side of things. They are also ridiculously cheap: A Venice–Verona second-class R or RV (there's no difference in practice) ticket will put you back only 8.60€ compared with 23€ on the Frecciabianca. You can't prebook seats on R or RV services, nor is there any price advantage to booking tickets ahead of travel.

Overcrowding is often a problem on standard services (that is, not the high-speed trains) Friday evenings, weekends, and holidays, especially in or out of big cities, or just after a strike. In summer, the crowding escalates, and any train going toward a beach in August bulges like an overstuffed sausage.

Train Travel Tips When buying a regular ticket, ask for either *andata* (one-way) or *andata e ritorno* (round-trip). The best way to avoid presenting yourself on the train with the wrong ticket is to tell the person at the ticket window exactly what train you are going to take, for example, "the 11:30am train for Venice." Regular R or RV tickets are not valid on high-speed trains.

If you don't have a ticket with a reservation for a particular seat on a specific train, then you must **validate you ticket by stamping it in the little yellow box** on the platform before boarding the train. If you board a train without a ticket, or without having validated your ticket, you'll have to pay a hefty fine on top of the ticket or supplement, which the conductor will sell you. If you knowingly board a train without a ticket or realize once onboard that you have the wrong type of ticket, your best bet is to search out the conductor, who is likely to be more forgiving because you found him and made it clear you weren't trying to ride for free.

Schedules for all trains leaving a given station are printed on yellow posters tacked up on the station wall (a similar white poster lists all the arrivals). These are good for getting general guidance, but keep your eye on the electronic boards and television screens that are updated with delays and track (*binario*) changes. You can also get official schedules (plus more train information, also in English) and buy tickets at both www.trenitalia.com and **www.italotreno.it**.

In the big cities (especially Milan and Rome) and major tourist destinations (above all Venice and Florence), ticketing lines can be dreadfully long. Don't be scared of the **automatic ticket machines.** They are easy to navigate, allow you to follow instructions in English, accept cash and credit cards, and can considerably cut down the stress of waiting in an interminably slow line. ***Note:*** You can't buy international tickets at automatic machines.

Stations tend to be well run, with luggage storage facilities at all but the smallest and usually a good bar attached that serves surprisingly palatable food. If you pull into a dinky town with a shed-size station, find the nearest bar or *tabacchi,* and the man behind the counter will most likely sell tickets.

SPECIAL PASSES & DISCOUNTS   To buy the **Eurail Italy Pass,** available only outside Europe and priced in U.S. dollars, contact **Rail Europe** (www.rail europe.com). You have 1 month in which to use the train a set number of days; the base number of days is 3, and you can add up to 5 more. For adults, the first-class pass costs $222, second class is $179. Additional days cost $30 to $35 more for first class, roughly $25 for second class. For youth tickets (25 and under), a 3-day pass is $179/$146 and additional days about $20 each. Saver passes are available for groups of two to five people traveling together **at all times,** and amount to a saving of about 15% on individual tickets.

When it comes to regular tickets, if you're **25 and under,** you can buy a 40€ **Carta Verde (Green Card)** at any Italian train station. This gets you a 10% break on domestic trips (walk-up fares only) and 25% off international connections for 1 year. Present it each time you buy a ticket. An even better deal is available for anyone **61 and over** with the **Carta d'Argento**

Travel Times Between the Major Cities

CITIES	DISTANCE	(FASTEST) TRAIN TRAVEL TIME	DRIVING TIME
Florence to Milan	298km/185 miles	1 hr., 40 min.	3½ hr.
Milan to Venice	267km/166 miles	2¼ hr.	3¼ hr.
Milan to Rome	572km/355 miles	2 hr., 55 min.	5½ hr.
Rome to Turin	669km/415 miles	4 hr.	6½ hr.

(Silver Card): 15% off domestic walk-up fares and 25% off international, for 30€ (the Carta d'Argento is free for those 76 and over). Children 11 and under ride half-price while kids under 4 don't pay, although they also do not have the right to their own seat. On state railways, there are sometimes free tickets for children 14 and under traveling with a paying adult; ask about "Bimbi gratis" when buying your ticket.

By Bus

Although trains are quicker and easier, you can get just about anywhere on a network of local, provincial, and regional bus lines. Keep in mind that in smaller towns, buses exist mainly to shuttle workers and school-children, so the most runs are on weekdays, early in the morning, and usually again in midafternoon.

In a big city, the **bus station** for trips between cities is usually near the main train station. A small town's **bus stop** is usually either in the main square, on the edge of town, or the bend in the road just outside the main town gate. You should always try to find the local ticket vendor—if there's no office, it's invariably the nearest newsstand or *tabacchi* (signaled by a sign with a white t), or occasionally a bar—but you can usually also buy tickets on the bus. You can sometimes flag down a bus as it passes on a country road, but try to find an official stop (a small sign tacked onto a telephone pole). Tell the driver where you're going and ask him courteously if he'll let you know when you need to get off. When he says, *"È la prossima fermata,"* that means yours is the next stop. *"Posso scendere a...?"* (*Poh*-so *shen*-dair-ay ah...?) is "Can I get off at...?"

[FastFACTS] ITALY

Area Codes The **country code** for Italy is **39.** Former **city codes** (for example, Florence 055, Venice 041, Milan 02, Rome 06) are incorporated into the numbers themselves. Therefore, you must dial the entire number, ***including the initial zero,*** when calling from *anywhere* outside or inside Italy and even within the same town. For example, to call Milan from the United States, you must dial **011-39-02,** then the local phone number. Phone numbers in Italy can range anywhere from 6 to 12 digits in length.

ATMs The easiest and best way to get cash away from home is from an ATM (automated teller machine), referred to in Italy as a **bancomat.** ATMs are prevalent in Italian cities and while every town usually has one, it's good practice to fuel up on cash in urban centers before traveling to villages or rural areas.

Be sure to confirm with your bank that your card is valid for international withdrawal and that you have a four-digit PIN. (Some ATMs in Italy will not accept any other number of digits.) Also, be sure you know your daily withdrawal limit before you depart. **Note:** Many banks impose a fee every time you use a card at another bank's ATM, and that fee can be higher for international transactions (up to $5 or more) than for domestic ones. In addition, the bank from which you withdraw cash may charge its own fee, although this is not common practice in Italy.

Business Hours General open hours for **stores, offices,** and **churches** are from 9:30am to noon or 1pm and again from 3 or 3.30pm to 7.30 or 8pm. The early afternoon shutdown is the *riposo,* the Italian siesta (in the downtown area of large cities, stores don't close for the *riposo*). Most stores close all day Sunday and many also on Monday (morning only or all day). Some services and business offices are open to the public only in the morning. **Banks** tend to be open Monday through Friday 8:30am to 1:30pm and 2:45 to 4:15pm. Traditionally, **state museums** are closed Mondays. Most of the large museums stay open all day long otherwise, although some close for *riposo* or are only open in the morning (9am–2pm is popular). Some churches open earlier in the morning, and the largest often stay open all day, though the last hour or so of opening is usually taken up with an evening service, during which tourist visits are frowned upon.

Customs   Foreign visitors can bring along most items for personal use duty-free, including merchandise valued up to $800.

Disabled Travelers   A few of the top museums and churches have installed ramps at their entrances, and several hotels have converted first-floor rooms into accessible units. Other than that, you may not find parts of Italy easy to tackle. Builders in the Middle Ages and the Renaissance didn't have wheelchairs or mobility impairments in mind when they built narrow doorways and spiral staircases, and preservation laws prevent Italians from doing much about this in some areas.

Some buses and trains can cause problems as well, with high, narrow doors and steep steps at entrances—though the situation on public transportation, especially the railways, is improving. For those with disabilities who can make it onto buses and trains, there are usually seats reserved for them, and Italians are quick to give up their space for somebody who looks like they need it more than them.

Accessible Italy (www.accessibleitaly.com; **(** **378-0549-941-111**) provides travelers with info about accessible tourist sites and places to rent wheelchairs, and also sells organized "Accessible Tours" around Italy. Disabled travelers should call **Trenitalia** (**(** **199-303060**) for assistance on the state rail network. Italo has a couple of dedicated wheelchair spaces on every service: Call **(** **06-07-08.**

Drinking Laws   People of any age can legally consume alcohol in Italy, but a person must be 16 years old in order to be served alcohol in a restaurant or a bar. Noise is the primary concern to city officials, and so bars generally close around 2am, though alcohol is commonly served in clubs after that. Supermarkets carry beer, wine, and spirits.

Electricity   Italy operates on a 220-volt AC (50 cycles) system, as opposed to the U.S. 110-volt AC (60 cycles) system. You'll need a simple adapter plug to make the American flat pegs fit the Italian round holes and, unless your appliance is dual-voltage (as some hair dryers, travel irons, and almost all laptops are), an electrical currency converter. You can pick up the hardware at electronics stores, luggage shops, and airports.

Embassies & Consulates   The **U.K. Embassy** (www.gov.uk/government/world/italy.it; ✆ **06-4220-0001**) is in Rome at Via XX Settembre 80a. The **British Consulate-General** is in Milan at Via San Paolo 7 (✆ **02-7230-0237**).

The **U.S. Embassy** is in Rome at Via Vittorio Veneto 121 (http://italy.usembassy.gov; ✆ **06-46-741**). There are also **U.S. Consulates General** in **Florence,** at Lungarno Vespucci 38 (http://florence.usconsulate.gov; ✆ **055-266-951**); in **Milan,** at Via Principe Amedeo 2/10 (http://milan.usconsulate.gov; ✆ **02-290-351**); and in **Naples,** in Piazza della Repubblica (http://naples.usconsulate.gov; ✆ **081-583-8111**).

Emergencies   The best number to call in Italy (and the rest of Europe) with a **general emergency** is ✆ **112,** which connects you to the **carabinieri** who will transfer your call as needed. For the **police,** dial ✆ **113;** for a **medical emergency** and to call an **ambulance,** the number is ✆ **118;** for the **fire department,** call ✆ **115.** If your car breaks down, dial ✆ **116** for **roadside aid** courtesy of the Automotive Club of Italy. All are free calls, but roadside assistance is a paid-for service for nonmembers.

Family Travel   Italy is a family-oriented society. A crying baby at a dinner table is greeted with a knowing smile rather than with a stern look. Children almost always receive discounts, and maybe a special treat from the waiter, but the availability of such accoutrements as child seats for cars and dinner tables is more the exception than the norm. (The former, however, is a legal requirement: Be sure to ask a rental car company to provide one.) There are plenty of parks, offbeat museums, markets, ice-cream parlors, and vibrant street-life scenes to amuse even the youngest children. Child discounts apply on public transportation, and at public and private museums. **Prénatal** (www.prenatal.com) is the premier toddler and baby chain store in Italy.

Health   You won't encounter any special health risks by visiting Italy. The country's public health care system is generally well regarded. The richer north tends to have better **hospitals** than the south.

Italy offers universal health care to its citizens and those of other European Union countries (U.K. nationals should remember to carry an EHIC: See **www.nhs.uk/ehic**). Others should be prepared to pay medical bills upfront. Before leaving home, find out what medical services your **health insurance** covers. *Note:* Even if you don't have insurance, you will always be treated in an emergency room.

Pharmacies offer essentially the same range of generic drugs available in the United States and internationally. Pharmacies are ubiquitous (look for the green cross) and serve almost like miniclinics, where pharmacists diagnose and treat minor ailments, like flu symptoms and general aches and pains, with over-the-counter drugs. Carry the generic name of any prescription medicines you take, in case a local pharmacist is unfamiliar with the brand name. Pharmacies in cities take turns doing the night shift; normally there is a list posted at the entrance of each pharmacy informing customers which pharmacy is open each night of the week.

Insurance   Italy may be one of the safer places you can travel in the world, but accidents and setbacks can and do happen, from lost luggage to car crashes. For information on traveler's insurance, trip cancellation insurance, and medical insurance while traveling, please visit **www.frommers.com/tips**.

Internet Access   Internet cafes are in healthy supply in most Italian cities, though don't expect to find them in every small town. If you're traveling with your own computer or smartphone, you'll find wireless access in almost every hotel, but if this is essential for your stay make sure you ask before booking and certainly don't always expect to find a connection in a rural *agriturismo* (disconnecting from the 21st century is part of their appeal). In a pinch, hostels, local libraries, and some bars will have some sort of terminal for access. Several spots around Venice, Florence, Rome, and other big cities are covered with free Wi-Fi access provided by the local administration, but at these and any other Wi-Fi spots around Italy, antiterrorism laws make it obligatory to register for an access code before you can log on. Take your passport or other photo ID when you go looking for an Internet point.

LGBT Travelers   Italy as a whole, and northern Italy in particular, is gay-friendly. Homosexuality is legal, and the age of consent is

16. Italians are generally more affectionate and physical than North Americans in all their friendships, and even straight men occasionally walk down the street with their arms around each other—however, kissing anywhere other than on the cheeks at greetings and goodbyes will draw attention. As you might expect, smaller towns tend to be less permissive than cities.

Italy's national associations and support networks for gays and lesbians are **ARCI-Gay and ArciLesbica.** The national websites are **www.arcigay.it** and **www.arcilesbica.it**, and most sizable cities have a local office (although not Venice). In **Verona,** the office is at Via Nichesola 9 (www.arcigayverona.org; ℰ **346-979-0553**); in **Milan,** Via Bezzecca 3 (www.arcigaymilano.org, ℰ **02-5412-2225**), and in **Rome,** Via Zabaglia 14 (www.arcigayroma.lt; ℰ **06-6450-1102**). See **www.arcigay.it/comitati** for a searchable directory.

Mail & Postage Sending a postcard or letter up to 20 grams, or a little less than an ounce, costs .95€ to other European countries, 2.30€ to North America, and a whopping 3€ to Australia and New Zealand. Full details on Italy's postal services are available at **www.poste.it** (some in English).

Mobile Phones **GSM** (Global System for Mobile Communications) is a cellphone technology used by most of the world's countries that makes it possible to turn on a phone with a contract based in Australia, Ireland, the U.K., Pakistan, or almost every other corner of the world and have it work in Italy without missing a beat. (In the U.S., service providers like Sprint and Verizon use a different technology—CDMA—and phones on those networks won't work in Italy unless they also have GSM compatibility.)

Also, if you are coming from the U.S. or Canada, you may need a multiband phone. All travelers should activate "international roaming" on their account, so check with your home service provider before leaving.

But—and it's a *big* but—using roaming can be very expensive, especially if you access the Internet on your phone. It is usually much cheaper, once you arrive, to buy an Italian SIM card (the removable plastic card found in all GSM phones that is encoded with your phone number). This is not difficult, and is an especially good idea if you will be in Italy for more than a week. You can **buy a SIM card** at one of the many cellphone shops you will pass in every city. The main service providers are TIM, Vodafone, Wind, and 3 *(Tre)*. If you have an Italian SIM card in your phone, local calls may be as low as .10€ per minute, and incoming calls are free. Value prepaid data packages are available for each, as are micro- and nano-SIMs, as well as prepaid deals for iPads and other tablets. If you need 4G data speeds, you will pay a little more. Not every network allows **tethering**—be sure to ask if you need it. Deals on each network change regularly; for the latest see the website of one of this guide's authors: **www.donaldstrachan.com/dataroaming italy**. *Note:* Contract cellphones are often "locked" and will only work with a SIM card provided by the service provider back home, so check to see that you have an unlocked phone.

Buying a phone is another option, and you shouldn't have too much trouble finding one for about 30€. Use it, then recycle it or eBay it when you get home. It will save you a fortune versus alternatives such as roaming or using hotel room telephones.

Money & Costs

Frommer's lists exact prices in the local currency. The currency conversions quoted below were correct at press time. However, rates fluctuate, so before departing, consult a currency exchange website, such as **www.oanda.com/convert/classic**, to check up-to-the-minute rates.

Like many European countries, Italy uses the euro as its currency. Euro coins are issued in denominations of .01€, .02€, .05€, .10€, .20€, and .50€, as well as 1€ and 2€; bills come in denominations of 5€, 10€, 20€, 50€, 100€, 200€, and 500€.

The evolution of international computerized banking and consolidated ATM networks has led to the triumph of plastic throughout the Italian peninsula—even if cold cash is still the most trusted currency in mom-and-pop joints. However, it is always a good idea to carry some cash, as small businesses may accept only cash or may claim that their credit card machine is broken to avoid paying fees to the card companies. Traveler's checks have gone the way of the Stegosaurus.

You'll get the best rate if you **exchange money** at a bank or one of its ATMs. The rates at "cambio/change/wechsel" exchange booths are invariably less favorable but still better than what you'd get exchanging money at a hotel or shop (a last-resort tactic only).

Money & Costs

PLANNING

Visa and **MasterCard** are almost universally accepted. Some businesses also take **American Express,** especially at the higher end, but few take **Diners Club.**

Finally, be sure to let your bank know that you will be traveling abroad to avoid having your card blocked after a few days of big purchases far from home. ***Note:*** Many banks assess a 1% to 3% "transaction fee" on **all** charges you incur abroad (whether you're using the local currency or your native currency).

Police   For emergencies, call 📞 **112** or 📞 **113.** Italy has several different police forces, but there are only two you'll most likely ever need to deal with. The first is the *carabinieri* (📞 **112**), who normally only concern themselves with serious crimes, but point you in the right direction. The *polizia* (📞 **113**), whose city headquarters is called the *questura*, is the place to go for help with lost and stolen property or petty crimes.

Safety   Italy is a remarkably safe country. The worst threats you'll likely face are the pickpockets who sometimes frequent touristy areas and public buses; keep your hands on your camera at all times and your valuables in an under-the-clothes money belt or inside zip-pocket. Don't leave anything valuable in a rental car overnight, and leave nothing visible in it at any time. If you are robbed, you can fill out paperwork at the nearest police station *(questura)*, but this is mostly for insurance purposes or to get a new passport issued—don't expect them to spend any resources hunting down the perpetrator. In general, avoid public parks at night. The areas around city rail stations are often unsavory, but rarely worse than that. Otherwise, there's a real sense of personal security for travelers in Italy.

Senior Travel   Seniors and older people are treated with a great deal of respect and deference, but there are few specific programs, associations, or concessions made for them. The one exception is on admission prices for museums and sights, where those ages 60 or 65 and older will often get in at a reduced rate or even free. There are also special train passes and reductions on bus tickets and the like in many towns (see "Getting Around," p. 188). As a senior in Italy, you're *un anziano* or if you're a woman, *un'anziana,* "elderly"—it's a term of respect, and you should let people know you're one if you think a discount may be in order.

Smoking   Smoking has been eradicated from inside restaurants, bars, and most hotels, so smokers tend to take outside tables at bars and restaurants. If you're keen for an alfresco table, you are essentially choosing a seat in the smoking section; requesting that your neighbor not smoke may not be politely received.

Student Travelers   An **International Student Identity Card (ISIC)** qualifies students for savings on rail passes, plane tickets, entrance fees, and more. The card is valid for 1 year. You can apply for the card online at **www.myisic.com** or in person at **STA Travel** (www.statravel.com; ☏ **800/781-4040** in North America). If you're no longer a student but are still 26 and under, you can get an **International Youth Travel Card (IYTC)** and an **International Teacher Identity Card (ITIC)** from the same agency, either of which entitles you to some discounts. Students will also find that many university cities offer ample student discounts and inexpensive youth hostels.

Taxes   There's no sales tax added onto the price tag of purchases in Italy, but there is a 22% value-added tax (in Italy: IVA) automatically included in just about everything except basic foodstuffs like milk and bread. Entertainment, transport, hotels, and dining are among a group of goods taxed at a lower rate of 10%. For major purchases, you can get IVA refunded.

Tipping   In **hotels,** service is usually included in your bill. In family-run operations, additional tips are unnecessary and sometimes considered rude. In fancier places with a hired staff, however, you may want to leave a .50€ daily tip for the maid and pay the bellhop or porter 1€ per bag. In **restaurants,** a 1€ to 3€ per person "cover charge" is automatically added to the bill and in some tourist areas, especially Venice, another 10 to 15% is tacked on (except in the most unscrupulous of places, this will be noted on the menu somewhere; if unsure you should ask, *è incluso il servizio?*). It is not necessary to leave any extra money on the table, though it is not uncommon to leave up to 5€, especially for good service. Locals generally leave nothing. At **bars and cafes,** you can leave something very small on the counter for the barman (maybe 1€ if you have had several drinks), though it is not expected; there is no need to leave anything extra if you sit at a table, as they are likely already charging you double or triple the price you'd have paid standing at the bar. It is not necessary to tip **taxi** drivers, though it is common to round up the bill to the nearest euro or two.

Toilets Aside from train stations, where they cost about .50€ to use, and gas/petrol stations, where they are free (with perhaps a basket seeking donations), public toilets are few and far between. Standard procedure is to enter a cafe, make sure the bathroom is not *fuori servizio* (out of order), and then order a cup of coffee before bolting to the facilities.

USEFUL ITALIAN PHRASES

English	Italian	Pronunciation
Thank you	Grazie	**graht-tzee-yey**
You're welcome	Prego	**prey-go**
Please	Per favore	**pehr fah-vohr-eh**
Yes	Sì	**see**
No	No	**noh**
Good morning or Good day	Buongiorno	**bwohn-djor-noh**
Good evening	Buona sera	**bwohn-ah say-rah**
Good night	Buona notte	**bwohn-ah noht-tay**
It's a pleasure to meet you.	Piacere di conoscerla.	**pyah-cheh-reh dee koh-nohshehr-lah**
My name is ___.	Mi chiamo ___.	**mee kyah-moh**
And yours?	E lei?	**eh lay**
Do you speak English?	Parla inglese?	**pahr-lah een-gleh-seh**
How are you?	Come sta?	**koh-may stah**
Very well	Molto bene	**mohl-toh behn-ney**
Goodbye	Arrivederci	**ahr-ree-vah-dehr-chee**
Excuse me (to get attention)	Scusi	**skoo-zee**
Excuse me (to get past someone)	Permesso	**pehr-mehs-soh**

GETTING AROUND

English	Italian	Pronunciation
Where is . . . ?	Dovè . . . ?	*doh*-vey
the station	la stazione	lah stat-tzee-*oh*-neh
a hotel	un albergo	oon ahl-*behr*-goh
a restaurant	un ristorante	oon reest-ohr-*ahnt*-eh
the bathroom	il bagno	eel *bahn*-nyoh
I am looking for . . .	Cerco . . .	*chehr*-koh
the check-in counter	il check-in	eel check-in
the ticket counter	la biglietteria	*lah beel-lyeht-teh-ree-ah*
arrivals	l'area arrivi	*lah*-reh-ah ahr-*ree*-vee
departures	l'area partenze	*lah*-reh-ah pahr-*tehn*-tseh
gate number	l'uscita numero	loo-*shee*-tah *noo*-meh-roh
the restroom	la toilette	lah twa-*leht*
the police station	la stazione di polizia	lah stah-*tsyoh*-neh dee poh-lee-*tsee*-ah
the smoking area	l'area fumatori	*lah*-reh-ah foo-mah-*toh*-ree
the information booth	l'ufficio informazioni	loof-*fee*-choh een-*fohr*-mah-*tsyoh*-nee
a public telephone	un telefono pubblico	oon teh-*leh*-foh-noh *poob*-blee-koh
an ATM/cashpoint	un bancomat	oon *bahn*-koh-maht
baggage claim	il ritiro bagagli	eel ree-*tee*-roh bah-*gahl*-lyee
a cafe	un caffè	oon kahf-*feh*
a restaurant	un ristorante	oon ree-stoh-*rahn*-teh
a bar	un bar	oon bar
a bookstore	una libreria	*oo*-nah lee-breh-*ree*-ah

To the left	A sinistra	ah see-*nees*-tra
To the right	A destra	ah *dehy*-stra
Straight ahead	Avanti (*or* sempre diritto)	ahv-*vahn*-tee (*sehm*-pray dee-*reet*-toh)

DINING

English	Italian	Pronunciation
Breakfast	Prima colazione	*pree*-mah coh-laht-tzee-*ohn*-ay
Lunch	Pranzo	*prahn*-zoh
Dinner	Cena	*chay*-nah
How much is it?	Quanto costa?	*kwan*-toh *coh*-sta
The check, please	Il conto, per favore	eel kon-toh *pehr* fah-*vohr*-eh

A MATTER OF TIME

English	Italian	Pronunciation
When?	Quando?	*kwan*-doh
Yesterday	Ieri	ee-*yehr*-ree
Today	Oggi	*oh*-jee
Tomorrow	Domani	doh-*mah*-nee
What time is it?	Che ore sono?	kay *or*-ay *soh*-noh
It's one o'clock.	È l'una.	*eh loo*-nah
It's two o'clock.	Sono le due.	*soh*-noh leh *doo*-eh
It's two-thirty.	Sono le due e mezzo.	*soh*-noh leh *doo*-eh eh *mehd*-dzoh
It's noon.	È mezzogiorno.	*eh* mehd-dzoh-*johr*-noh
It's midnight.	È mezzanotte.	*eh* mehd-dzah-*noht*-teh
in the morning	al mattino	ahl maht-*tee*-noh
in the afternoon	al pomeriggio	ahl poh-meh-*reed*-joh
at night	alla notte	dee *noht*-the

DAYS OF THE WEEK

English	Italian	Pronunciation
Monday	Lunedì	**loo-nay-*dee***
Tuesday	Martedì	**mart-ay-*dee***
Wednesday	Mercoledì	**mehr-cohl-ay-*dee***
Thursday	Giovedì	**joh-vay-*dee***
Friday	Venerdì	**ven-nehr-*dee***
Saturday	Sabato	***sah*-bah-toh**
Sunday	Domenica	**doh-*mehn*-nee-kah**

MONTHS & SEASONS

English	Italian	Pronunciation
January	gennaio	**jehn-*nah*-yoh**
February	febbraio	**fehb-*brah*-yoh**
March	marzo	***mahr*-tso**
April	aprile	**ah-*pree*-leh**
May	maggio	***mahd*-joh**
June	giugno	***jewn*-nyo**
English	**Italian**	**Pronunciation**
July	luglio	***lool*-lyo**
August	agosto	**ah-*gohs*-toh**
September	settembre	**seht-*tehm*-breh**
October	ottobre	**oht-*toh*-breh**
November	novembre	**noh-*vehm*-breh**
December	dicembre	**dee-*chehm*-breh**
spring	la primavera	**lah pree-mah-*veh*-rah**
summer	l'estate	**lehs-*tah*-teh**
autumn	l'autunno	**low-*toon*-noh**
winter	l'inverno	**leen-*vehr*-noh**

NUMBERS

English	Italian	Pronunciation
1	uno	**oo-noh**
2	due	**doo-ay**
3	tre	**tray**
4	quattro	**kwah-troh**
5	cinque	**cheen-kway**
6	sei	**say**
7	sette	**set-tay**
8	otto	**oh-toh**
9	nove	**noh-vay**
10	dieci	**dee-ay-chee**
11	undici	**oon-dee-chee**
20	venti	**vehn-tee**
21	ventuno	**vehn-toon-oh**
22	venti due	**vehn-tee doo-ay**
30	trenta	**trayn-tah**
40	quaranta	**kwah-rahn-tah**
50	cinquanta	**cheen-kwan-tah**
60	sessanta	**sehs-sahn-tah**
70	settanta	**seht-tahn-tah**
80	ottanta	**oht-tahn-tah**
90	novanta	**noh-vahnt-tah**
100	cento	**chen-toh**
1,000	mille	**mee-lay**
5,000	cinque milla	**cheen-kway mee-lah**
10,000	dieci milla	**dee-ay-chee mee-lah**

Index

Accommodations

217

Restaurants

PHOTO CREDITS